WOMEN'S SOCIAL ENTREPRENEURSHIP

Women's social entrepreneurship has been proved to alleviate poverty and in parallel to promote gender equality. This book introduces a useful analysis of the field, investigating the emerging phenomenon of women's social entrepreneurship from both a conceptual and empirical perspective. The book is based on the premise that how gender is articulated within the entrepreneurial debate has to acknowledge context. Seven case studies are presented and, through them, the importance of women's social entrepreneurship for job creation is revealed. A complemented layout of activities is also provided to reinforce the business spirit of women's social entrepreneurship. Finally, the book provides suggestions and educational programmatical alterations for policy makers, which are needed to be invoked for the endorsement of women's social entrepreneurship. This book will be of interest to undergraduate and postgraduate students who study social entrepreneurship, to social entrepreneurship scholars and to the international academic library market in particular.

Panagiotis Kyriakopoulos is a Research Fellow at the Warwick Business School in the United Kingdom. He holds a Ph.D. in International Business from Adam Smith Business School – University of Glasgow, a Master's degree in International Management from Strathclyde Business School, and a Bachelor's degree in Business Administration and Management from Athens University of Economics and Business.

Routledge Focus on Business and Management

The fields of business and management have grown exponentially as areas of research and education. This growth presents challenges for readers trying to keep up with the latest important insights. *Routledge Focus on Business and Management* presents small books on big topics and how they intersect with the world of business research.

Individually, each title in the series provides coverage of a key academic topic, whilst collectively, the series forms a comprehensive collection across the business disciplines.

Gender Diversity and Inclusion at Work
Divergent Views from Turkey
Zeynep Özsoy, Mustafa Şenyücel and Beyza Oba

Management and Visualisation
Seeing Beyond the Strategic
Gordon Fletcher

Knowledge Management and AI in Society 5.0
Manlio Del Giudice, Veronica Scuotto and Armando Papa

The Logistics Audit
Methods, Organization and Practice
Piotr Buła and Bartosz Niedzielski

Women's Social Entrepreneurship
Case Studies from the United Kingdom
Panagiotis Kyriakopoulos

For more information about this series, please visit: www.routledge.com/ Routledge-Focus-on-Business-and-Management/book-series/FBM

Women's Social Entrepreneurship

Case Studies from the United Kingdom

Panagiotis Kyriakopoulos

Routledge
Taylor & Francis Group

NEW YORK AND LONDON

First published 2023
by Routledge
605 Third Avenue, New York, NY 10158

and by Routledge
4 Park Square, Milton Park, Abingdon, Oxon, OX14 4RN

Routledge is an imprint of the Taylor & Francis Group, an informa business

ISBN: 978-1-032-52421-4 (hbk)
ISBN: 978-1-032-52571-6 (pbk)
ISBN: 978-1-003-40724-9 (ebk)

DOI: 10.4324/9781003407249

Typeset in Times New Roman
by codeMantra

Dedicated to my family, and
my Professor Pavlos Dimitratos who left us early.

Contents

About the author

Dr. Panagiotis Kyriakopoulos is a Research Fellow at the Warwick Business School in the United Kingdom. He holds a Ph.D. in International Business from Adam Smith Business School – University of Glasgow, a Master's degree in International Management from Strathclyde Business School, and a Bachelor's degree in Business Administration and Management from Athens University of Economics and Business. He served as a visiting researcher at the University of Dundee – Dundee Business School in the United Kingdom, at Technologico de Monterrey in Mexico and at NEOMA Business School in France. He has received the highest scores among all graduates at both undergraduate and postgraduate level (valedictorian). His master's thesis was characterised as "Outstanding" and was awarded as the best thesis of the postgraduate programme. His research interests include technology parks, social entrepreneurship, internationalisation of small and medium-sized enterprises, international entrepreneurship and international business strategy.

He has won the Adam Smith Business School Award for Excellence in Research (Management) for two consecutive years (2021 and 2022), and the Business and Innovation Award at the Study UK Alumni Awards 2022. He was also granted honorary awards of academic performance from the Foundation for Education and European Culture, the Alexander Onassis Foundation and other foundations. He has worked at the US multinational company Marsh & McLennan Companies and the Intrakat Group (Intracom Holdings). He has participated in a plethora of scientific conferences and has published his research in reputed publishers of academic books including Edward Elgar and Routledge.

They said about the author

Angie De Vos – former CEO and President of Women's Business Station (WBS)

"My collaboration with Panagiotis for the creation of an economic and social tool for the social enterprise Women's Business Station (WBS) was particularly pleasant, productive and effective. Panagiotis, via a series of initiatives and his passion for women's entrepreneurship, guided the research effectively and permitted us to create a strong and friendly to the user tool of performance measurement which will aid us to the capitalization of the impact via an essential but also convincing way. I am certain that the social enterprise Women's Business Station has won a long-term friend and I am sincerely grateful for that. Thank you very much!"

Norin Arshed – Professor and Chair of Entrepreneurship, Associate Dean for Research & Knowledge at Dundee Business School of the United Kingdom

"My collaboration with Panagiotis was excellent as it contributed significantly to our research on how the social enterprise Women's Business Station (WBS) is able to ensure a future impact on other women who are occupied with women's social entrepreneurship. Panagiotis played a key role for the support of Women's Business Station via the creation of a series of suggestions and tools for the measurement of the social impact of the social enterprise by capitalizing its financial and social performance but also its institutional legitimacy".

Preface

It was the spring of 2021, when the University of Dundee in the United Kingdom invited me to be a member of a research programme relevant to women's entrepreneurship in the United Kingdom. The idea of studying the section of women's entrepreneurship for a developed economy such as the economy of the United Kingdom comprised a challenge for me and imminently accepted to join the research team of the University of Dundee.

As soon as I undertook the research for the women's entrepreneurship in the United Kingdom and met the Administrative Board of the first social enterprise the Women's Business Station (WBS), I confess that I was impressed by the social work that is being performed by this social enterprise. I confess that what impressed me more was the fact that this social enterprise had a strong social impact in society, beyond the benefits for the national economy. While researching in parallel the work that is being performed by this specific social enterprise (which is analysed in the continuance of the book) I decided to research on the other social enterprises that perform similar work and are also active in the United Kingdom.

Apprehending that the role of a researcher is, and should be, to share his scientific knowledge and give it back to the society, I decided to depict in a complemented book all the knowledge I accumulated during this research trip. Alongside, I would like to point out that this book is the result of hard effort and work at a period of my life that I had a great deal of research and teaching obligations.

Athens, September 10, 2023

Introduction

The present book introduces with a theoretical and practically useful analysis the emerging phenomenon of the women's social entrepreneurship. The women's social entrepreneurship has been proved to alleviate poverty and in parallel to promote gender equality. The conversation of the challenges of the women's entrepreneurship aims to the creation of a deeper understanding of the women's social entrepreneurship and aids the theoretical apprehension of this developing scientific section in a better way. For the purposes of the book, seven case studies from the United Kingdom were selected confirming the importance of the women's social entrepreneurship for job creation, which, in turn, may lead to the economic development of a country around the world. A complemented layout of activities is also provided to reinforce the business spirit of women's social entrepreneurship. Finally, the book provides a set of suggestions and educational-programmatical alterations for the administrators of policy makers and the professionals, which are needed to be invoked for the endorsement of the women's social entrepreneurship.

DOI: 10.4324/9781003407249-1

1 Theoretical part – women's social entrepreneurship

An emerging form of entrepreneurship

1.1 Introduction

In a constantly changing environment that the future of businesses may be uncertain, it is particularly important for businesses to create the opportunities of the future by themselves to succeed. In recent years, social entrepreneurship is particularly widespread in every country around the world, and it is dynamically growing. Going beyond revenue and profit could be quite important not only for understanding the different relationship among stakeholders (i.e., customers, local communities, employees) within an ecosystem, but also for exploring to what extent and how social enterprises generate new ideas, and provide solutions for social problems in a changing world. Creating social impact and social value is not only a priority for social enterprises, but also for-profit enterprises that include in their strategy corporate social responsibility (CSR) actions. However, although social entrepreneurship and CSR share come goals, they are quite different, since the former are proactive driving a social change, while the latter are focusing on how businesses may create a positive image contributing to social welfare (Bansal, Garg & Sharma, 2019). Indeed, the CSR actions include a series of actions, as for example, actions for the protection of the environment, educational support via scholarships, donations for the implementation of actions, actions relevant to the financial support of weak teams, but also various series of actions for the increase of the social value and the social impact. Besides, however, the increase of social actions from the for-profit enterprises, the appearance of social enterprises that aim to significantly increase the social value via the implementation of their main activities, is obvious.

In most countries, we may identify some successful and leading cases of social enterprises (or social organisations). Noticeably, for instance, the most impactful social organisation in Greece, is "Apostoli" (Mission) that aims to provide human support via dozens of actions. It was founded by the Archbishop of Athens and All Greece Ieronymos II and helps through several actions thousands of people (Apostoli, 2023a). The purpose of "Apostoli"

DOI: 10.4324/9781003407249-2

is charity and the relief of the weaker social teams via the improvement of their living conditions (Apostoli, 2023b). "Apostoli" accomplishes dozens of actions via social structures, as for example the Karelleio Standard Alzheimer Centre, the Hostel of Unaccompanied Refugee Minors "Estia", the Nursing Home for the Chronic Mental Patients at Kypseli, the Day Centre of Mental Health in Argostoli of Kefalonia, the Day Centre of Mental Health in Chios, the Day Centre of Mental Health in Ierapetra, the Day Centre of Mental Health in Neapolis in Crete, the Mobile Unit of Mental Health in Karditsa, the Mobile Unit of Mental Health in Sparta, the Supported Housing (S.H.) as well as the Protected Apartment. Alongside, "Apostoli" provides via the Social Mission Medical Centre, all the necessary medicine for the financially and socially weaker citizens (Apostoli, 2023c). Beyond the dozens of social structures, "Apostoli" provides Social Groceries in Kallithea, Lesvos, Moschato-Tavros, Daphne-Ymittos, N. Heraklion, Orestiada and also Preveza. The social work of "Apostoli" also includes a series of programmes for the enhancement of businesses and associations, the support of the unemployed, pupils and students also via educational programme such as "Demetrio" Centre of Children's Creative Work (CCCW) (Apostoli, 2023c).

The vision of "Apostoli" is the constant struggle to change the lives of the financially and socially weaker people, the insecurity, the uncertainty, the sadness, the despair and the hopelessness that a lot of our fellow human beings experience in order to find a shelter of understanding, affection, care and help via the social structures and actions of "Apostoli". The phrase, in which the vision of "Apostoli" is depicted, is typical: "None of our fellow human beings without food, roof, doctor and medicine" (Apostoli, 2023d).

The offering of this organisation has the greatest social impact in Greece at the moment; it is considered as saucerful case study at a global level of church can contribute to the wider community alleviating poverty as the number of the benefactors at pan-Hellenic level is impressive. More analytically, more than 166,407 packages have been delivered up today to pupils' families via school units, more than 2,000,000 drug formulations have been disposed to the frontier and remote areas and more than 324,736 food portions and packages of food emergency help have been offered for the feeding of the refugees at the hospitality centres. "Apostoli" is mainly supported by donations from third parties and the contribution of the ordinary people is particularly important for the continuation of its work (Apostoli, 2023d).

Another interesting case of social organisation in Greece which adopts the model of social offering is the social enterprise "Ithaca Laundry" which was founded in 2015 and has as a target the provision of clothes cleaning services (via a mobile unit of washing machines) to people who do not have the financial capacity to support the washing of their clothes, either because they are homeless or because they simply cannot afford it. A basic belief of "Ithaca Laundry" is that: "Cleanness leads to dignity and dignity, in turn, to new opportunities" (Ithaca, 2023a). More analytically, the action of "Ithaca Laundry" aims at the social rehabilitation of people from vulnerable population groups. Since 2016, the actions of "Ithaca Laundry" have ensured hygiene conditions to people who are in need. In the frame of these actions, alongside with the hygiene services, "Ithaca" has created various work-employment places for people who come from vulnerable social groups, and it has helped over 8,000 people (Ithaca, 2023b).

A key social non-partisan Non-Governmental Organization (NGO) in Greece supporting equal opportunities for all is "Women Act" that aims to empower women to fully embrace their political, social, cultural and economic potential by actively participating in the public sphere (Women Act, 2023a). It was created in 2017, and it aims to foster a truly equal society decreasing the women under-participation in decision-making. It empowers women in leadership roles and their participation in local, regional and international authorities around the world through a series of activities (i.e., leadership academy, workshops, events, partnerships with leading companies, panel discussions, aperitifs) (Women Act, 2023b). Promoting women as leaders of change in the public sphere, it offers a set of skills that allow women to hone their leadership skills raising their awareness on gender equality issues. It is also interesting that the vision of "Women Act" is to have a world where the participation of women will be equal to men in the public activities "Planet 50-50 by 2030" decreasing any gender equality gap (Women Act, 2023c).

Another interesting and impactful initiative of Women Act is the initiative "No More Manels" fostering the principles of inclusion and diversity. Specifically, it aims to increase the level of awareness regarding the equal participation of women and men in different discussion of public debates (Women Act, 2023d). Last but not least, it has been developed through the initiative "No More Manels" a network of organisations (i.e., Hellenic Federation of Enterprises, LSE Alumni Association, Women on Top, diaNEOsis, The Hellenic Foundation for European and Foreign Policy, and many other organisations) (Women Act, 2023d).

In the recent years, it is apparent that the role of women in society has been gaining ground, and there is a rotation from women to create social enterprises. The increased unemployment in many European countries, has led a lot of women to discover other professional paths, beyond their employment in the private or public sector. Greece constitutes a particularly distressed country as she has recently been through a global economic crisis, beyond the health crisis of COVID-19, has also been through the economic crisis of 2009. Every crisis constitutes a threat for many enterprises as they close down, not being able to financially compensate for their obligations, but also constitutes an opportunity for others that locate, by any chance, opportunities and have the abilities to respond to the uncertainty of the outer environment.

1.2   Definition and characteristics of social entrepreneurship

The phenomenon of social entrepreneurship has existed for many decades and can take the form of an NGO which does not have the purpose of profit but of some public benefit purpose (Grenier, 2009). However, the concept of social entrepreneurship was also introduced in the late 1970s, via the establishment of small-credit institutions; however the term of social entrepreneurship has been established since the last 20–25 years (Grenier, 2009).

However, it is true that there is not a commonly accepted definition in the international bibliography for the concept of "social entrepreneurship", although many researchers agree to some of its characteristics (Teasdale, 2012). The researchers in the social entrepreneurship literature agree that, among others, some of the common characteristics of social entrepreneurship are moral social behaviour, creation of a social impact and innovation (Dacin, Dacin & Matear, 2010). Many researchers agree, also, that the social and environmental impacts are the main purposes of a social enterprise (Huybrechts & Nicholls, 2012). Moreover, the motivation of creating a social enterprise is social sensitivity which is depicted in the vision, the mission as well as the implementation of the aims of the social enterprise (Sastre-Castillo, Peris-Ortiz & Danvila-Del Valle, 2015). Indeed, a social enterprise generates positive social impact and environmental externalities (Santos, 2012).

It is also interesting that social entrepreneurs may demonstrate some unique (personal) characteristics compared to profit-oriented entrepreneurs, and there are some motivational reasons behind creating a social enterprise (Ghalwash, Tolba & Ismail, 2017). Indeed, the social entrepreneurs are characterised by their ability to co-operate with people from different social and cognitive backgrounds in order to solve a problem that frustrates society and create social value (Alter, 2006). The social entrepreneurs are also characterised by the accountability, unreasonableness and resourcefulness as money for them constitutes exclusively a means of implementing the social mission of their social enterprise generating social impact in the local and the wider community (Waddock & Post, 1991; Phills, Deiglmeier & Dale, 2008). Social entrepreneurs are usually proactive personalities revealing their tendency to influence environmental changes and maximising the chances of both financial and social performance (Manolopoulos, Salavou, Papadopoulos & Xenakis, 2022). The main motivation of a social entrepreneur is "philanthropy" or "altruism" creating social welfare (reducing income inequalities, poverty rates, etc.), and achieving social goals (Zahra, Gedajlovic, Neubaum, & Shulman, 2009).

1.3   Different business models of social enterprises

Social enterprises usually follow a different path to solve social problems producing triple bottom line (TBL): economic, social and environmental value and increasing collective wealth (Freeman & Reed, 1983; Elkington, 1998). To prioritise their TBL objectives, however, social enterprises need to adopt an effective business model fulfilling their social mission (Glavas & Mish, 2015). Although business models of social enterprises become even more significant for social enterprises, there is not an agreed definition (Yunus, Moingeon & Lehmann-Ortega, 2010). In general, business model is a process in which social enterprise creates, captures and delivers value to society via a series of activities (Tykkyläinen & Ritala, 2021). To have effectiveness of business models, however, we need to create value in different phases (i.e., identify value creation opportunities, refine a value creation process) (Sjödin, Parida, Jovanovic & Visnjic, 2020).

A social enterprise may generate many types of values; however, the main groups of values are three including social, economic and environmental. First of all, social value is created for a specific social group of people, and in this way, it may positively serve society. Value can be generated by social enterprise achieving a social change, and addressing social needs (Bocken, Short, Rana & Evans, 2014). Also, by creating social value, the restriction of exclusion of some social groups of the general population is implied who until recently were excluded or faced certain difficulties which held back their everyday life, as well as the whole quality of their everyday life (Cajaiba-Santana, 2014).

Additionally, another value category which can be created by a social enterprise is economic (or financial) value. Although a lot of the social enterprises decide to offer their product or their service for free and cover the expenses that are required for their creation by themselves via own resources – sponsorships, donations or grants – some other social enterprises decide to offer their product or service for some financial consideration. Although it is true that imposing some financial consideration is not a purpose in itself of the social enterprises, as they do not aim exclusively at the creation of economic value, and for this reason they differ from the for-profit lining enterprises companies that aim exclusively at profit. When the financial consideration exceeds the product or service cost, then the economic value is produced for the social enterprise (Chell, 2007). Last but not least, it is true that beyond the social and economic value that a social enterprise can create, the environmental value can also be produced with the purpose of the enhancement of the measures of environmental protection (Smith, 2014).

Although many social enterprises are focusing only to generate social value (or environmental value) and aiming only to get grants without generating any revenue from their core activities, there are other types of social enterprises that adopt a hybrid form (a combination of profit-seeking with an embedded social/environmental purpose), as we will present in the part B of this study. Indeed, more and more social enterprises tend to adopt a hybrid business model and, besides the social offering, have profit that re-invested for generating social or environmental impact. The hybrid business model of social entrepreneurship acquires more and more a greater importance for the social enterprises of today due to be self-sustainable rather than depending on any grants. For instance, the street magazine "Shedia" (The Raft), of NGO Diogenis which was established in 2010 is a social enterprise which hires unemployed people to sell the magazine for a fee, at various points of the city as for example outside train stations or at central streets (Shedia, 2023). The sale of the magazine for a fee makes the organisation adopt a hybrid entrepreneurship model as it has a two-fold purpose, the social offering as well as profit.

Value measurement (i.e., performance indicators) of social enterprises constitutes a particularly interesting research field that has attracted the attention of the social entrepreneurship literature (Rawhouser, Cummings & Newbert, 2019). According to the social entrepreneurship literature, for the value measurement of social enterprises the recording of resources required to produce products or services (i.e., any relevant costs, inputs and outputs, knowledge and experience) is needed. For social enterprises, it is crucial to identify and communicate to different stakeholders some key short-term results, such as how many people were benefited (found feeding, accommodation, etc.) or how many people were educated, how many infrastructures were created due to the social enterprise. Apart from, however, the short-term social impact generated by social enterprise, long-term benefits for society and economy may also be created. For instance, it is worth measuring how well the quality of living of a person may be improved or his income per capita (at individual level). At community level or ecosystem level, indicators relevant to the development of human progress or poverty reduction can be also achieved (Ebrahim & Rangan, 2014).

It should be noted, however, that business models in most cases include three main characteristics: (i) the value of product/service delivered to customers (value proposition), (ii) the way that social enterprise is structured/ organised (i.e., internal and external value chain, collaboration with partners) to deliver this value of product/service to customers (value constellation) and (iii) the revenue model according to which it generates value to the society (Yunus, Moingeon & Lehmann-Ortega, 2010).

Towards this direction, each social entrepreneur should take into account some considerations before deciding the type of business model. For instance, to create an effective value proposition, social enterprises may answer some of the following questions: Which are the main activities and the main product or service of social enterprise? At which section of the market does my social enterprise aim? How we generate value through our social enterprise? Who are our target customers? (Yunus, Moingeon & Lehmann-Ortega, 2010; Portales, 2019).

To address the second main characteristic of business model (i.e., value constellation), social enterprises need to address some of the following questions: Which are the networks of our partners that we can collaborate with to deliver value? Which are our key stakeholders (i.e., customers, local community), and how we can deliver value to them? Which is our main internal and external value chain that addresses a social need generating social value? Which are the distribution channels of the product or the service of my social enterprise? (Yunus, Moingeon & Lehmann-Ortega, 2010).

Regarding the third characteristic of business model for social enterprises, it mainly addresses how profit equation can be achieved (i.e., what are the main costs and revenues of social enterprises in order to generate social value). In particular, social enterprises may answer: What is the cost of the delivered product or service to customers? If I have profits from my social enterprise how and where from will be generated? (Osterwalder, Pigneur, Bernarda & Smith, 2014; Portales, 2019).

1.4   Selective differences between social enterprises and for-profit enterprises

Scanning the social entrepreneurship literature, we can see that the characteristics of a social enterprise and a for-profit enterprise may differ at various components. More analytically, a social enterprise is mainly driven by a social mission, which, in fact, includes the reason for its existence and all its activities are performed for the effective implementation of its (social) mission. On the other side, the mission and the vision of the "for- profit" enterprises are not (necessarily) driven by "philanthropy", and they may (possibly) not address a social challenge and or a problem (Zahra, Gedajlovic, Neubaum, & Shulman, 2009). The urge, that is, of the social enterprises lies in the change of the social conditions for solving a social problem (Choi & Majumdar, 2013). It is, also, important to be stressed that a social enterprise produces some social value apart from the economic value, reducing possible hindrance for some excluded social groups (Haigh, Walker, Bacq & Kickul, 2015). Finally, a social enterprise measures its success and effectiveness via indicators relevant to the social impact (i.e., reduction of poverty, improving access to wheelchairs and mobility equipment) and not via profitability and performance indicators (Peredo & McLean, 2006).

1.5   Leadership skills of social entrepreneurs

Leadership skills are considered as a key in the social entrepreneurship literature, and they refer to a set of strategic responses to environmental and situational turbulences (Ilac, 2018, p. 268). Given that leaders are driven by a social vision, they often demonstrate the ability to seize the opportunity in the macro-environment addressing a social need, adding social value through achieving a social change (Bocken, Short, Rana & Evans, 2014). Leadership skills are closely related to personal characteristics. For instance, leaders of social enterprises demonstrate self- awareness (authenticity), courage and calm, caring for others (Gravells, 2012). In addition, they often develop the ability to effectively communicate the vision and the mission of the social enterprise to stakeholders both internally and externally (Hall, Millo & Barman, 2015). Indeed, leaders of social enterprises should focus on a clear, regular and open communication of their social enterprise's values, and mission. All the employees of the social enterprise should believe in the mission and the vision of social enterprise to effectively conduct their everyday activities achieving the objectives of social enterprise.

The leadership skills of social entrepreneur are needed, however, not only at the process of creating a social enterprise, but also at the stage of its successful scaling. More specifically, the social entrepreneur needs to build a strong team in the early stages of social enterprise (i.e., founding team), but also to recruit, select, and retain employees sharing common values with social enterprise when they social enterprise scales (Ohana & Meyer, 2010; Godfroid, Otiti & Mersland, 2022). The social entrepreneur has also to identify, maintain and increase the number of the funder's network increasing the sustainability of social enterprise (Mizrahi & Rosenthal, 2001).

The leadership skills of social entrepreneur are also required at the process of adopting management systems that support the decentralised decision-making and provide many degrees of freedom to the employees of the social enterprise – for everyday simple issues – in order to accelerate decision making within the social enterprise, and for economic also reasons (Giudici, Combs, Cannatelli & Smith, 2020). Noticeably, the leadership skills are necessary for a social entrepreneur, not only during the creation of his social enterprise, but also during its scaling ensuring an effective response to organisational needs (Austin, Gutierrez, Ogliastri & Refcco, 2006).

1.6   Corporate social responsibility (CSR) of for-profit enterprises

CSR has drawn the interest of the researchers for decades as it does not constitute a new phenomenon for the entrepreneurship literature. Noticeably, more and more businesses tend to adopt a series of CSR activities responding to the increasing interest of stakeholders regarding social and environmental impact (Tate, Ellram & Kirchoff, 2010; Park, Kim & Kwon, 2017). Although there is not a single definition of the term CSR, they all agree that it includes a set of activities associated with social good, beyond the interests of firms and that which is required by law (McWilliams & Siegel, 2001; McWilliams, Siegel & Wright, 2006). Therefore, firms may use their internal resources to implement a series of activities to take advantage of a socially responsible image, which, in turn, may lead to a greater performance (either in an individual level or an organisational level) (Mishra & Suar, 2010).

More specifically, CSR could be crucial for-profit enterprises since it is positively associated with the (corporate) reputation, moral legitimacy, transparency, financial performance and environmental impact reducing environmental uncertainty (Park, Kim & Kwon, 2017; Kim, 2019). It could be also a useful practise for-profit enterprises since it may positively affect the purchase intention of customers, and their satisfaction (Carvalho, Sen, de Oliveira Mota & de Lima, 2010), while it could be beneficial for primary stakeholders (i.e., customers, employees, suppliers), but also for secondary stakeholders (media, local community, government, etc.) (Park, Chidlow & Choi, 2014).

CSR activities, for example, may include charity, grant scholarships to students, sponsorships, philanthropic contribution, donation of technological equipment to university students bringing the gap between employability and digital skills. Other CSR activities are also related to environmental responsibility, such as tree planting, energy efficiency, recycling, reuse and reduced carbon efficiency (Fallon, 2014). Some other for-profit enterprises, in cooperation with some public benefit institutions, can provide sponsorship for feeding or housing people who are in financial difficulty and are not able to cope with their everyday needs.

As it is understood, all the activities of CSR mainly concern for-profit enterprises, as they aim to create a good reputation responding to people's needs increasing their organisational credibility (Kim, 2019). Indeed, customers of products and services may perceive more ethical those for-profit enterprises with a great extent of CSR activities creating long-term relationships (Park, Kim & Kwon, 2017). In this way, the brand name and the brand image of company can be strengthened leading to higher revenues, and significantly improving firm's profitability (Gatti, Caruana & Snehota, 2012; Marques & Dhiman, 2020; Park & Park, 2021).

1.7 Women's social entrepreneurship in support of UN's 17 goals for sustainable development

Women's social entrepreneurship, besides the financial and social benefits that can bring upon a country, contributes to the goal achievement of UN. According to the Sustainable Development Goals (SDGs) Report (2019) of the United Nations (UN), the 17 sustainable goals of UN are the following (Sachs, Schmidt-Traub, Kroll, Lafortune & Fuller, 2019):

1 Poverty reduction.
2 Hunger reduction and improvement of nutritional conditions by promoting the sustainable rural sector.
3 Assurance of a qualitative and healthy way of living for all the people regardless their age.
4 Assurance of gender equality and reduction of any differences that lead to inequality, via promoting learning and educational opportunities.

5   Achievement of gender equality and reinforcement of women's and girls' role in society.
6   Assurance of water availability for all people.
7   Assurance of access to economic, reliable and sustainable energy for all.
8   Promotion of sustainable economic growth and productive work for all.
9   Building reliable infrastructures and empowerment of innovation.
10   Reduction of inequality among the countries.
11   Creation of safe and viable cities.
12   Responsible production and consumption.
13   Promotion of actions which contribute to the confrontation of climate change.
14   Promotion of actions for the assurance of the viability of oceans, seas and marine resources.
15   Protection and promotion of sustainable actions for the protection of forests and soil.
16   Promotion of actions for equality between societies and justice for all citizens.
17   Reinforcement of actions for the creation of global alliances for sustainable development.

As it is understood, based on the 17 UN goals, reinforcement of actions of women's entrepreneurship will contribute in its turn to the achievement of many UN goals. For instance, women's social entrepreneurship contributes to poverty reduction which constitutes the number one of the 17 UN goals, as new places of employment could be created and the Gross Domestic Product (GDP)[1] of every country could be increased. Bearing in mind that the GDP of every country constitutes the value of goods and services that are produced in each country, for a given time period (Barro, 2017), job creation may increase the number of people who can afford buying new products and services generating income for many people.

Additionally, it is understood that via the reinforcement of the women's social entrepreneurship, goal four of UN's 17 goals could be also achieved, as the wage gap between men and women could be softened and the opportunities for women to create their own enterprise (for-profit or social enterprise) could be increased. Reducing any wage gap between men and women, could be often achieved through the successful implementation via training courses, seminars and other educational activities to women raising the awareness of women entrepreneurship and breaking any gender stereotypes.

Alongside, however, goal five of the 17 UN's goals could be also achieved, as the reinforcement of women's entrepreneurship may contribute to the reinforcement of woman's role in the society, in general. Women's entrepreneurship, besides understanding various business terms, helps a woman gain income and be more active in the labour force than ever decreasing any economic exclusion due to their limited participation in the development of a society.

It is also impressive, that via women's social entrepreneurship, goal eight of UN's 17 goals could be also achieved. Economic development also comes via the creation of new enterprises (for- profit or social enterprises) and for this reason it is particularly significant to constitute a significant development pillar, the emphasis on entrepreneurship and the reduction in the obstacles which many times constitute an obstruction for the economic development of a country.

Last but not least, via women's social entrepreneurship goal 10 of UN's 17 goals could be also achieved. The reduction in inequality among the countries constitutes a significant goal of women's social entrepreneurship. Considering differences in the level of economic development of countries (i.e., some countries from advanced markets possess more financial resources to implement programmes for fostering women entrepreneurship), each country should pay attention to the reinforcement of social entrepreneurship creating an integrated framework about how women can create their own business reducing any obstacles (i.e., lack of information, knowledge).

1.8   Economic and social benefits from reinforcing women's (social or for-profit) entrepreneurship

The benefits from the women's social entrepreneurship are multiple for the national economy and the social cohesion of a country (Çingitaş & Sati, 2015). There are increasing data from the social entrepreneurship literature that the reinforcement of women's entrepreneurship has multiple benefits for society and the reduction in any inequalities that exist in many societies around the world (Wu, Wu & Sharpe, 2020). By reinforcing women's entrepreneurship, beyond the creation of social value, a number of economic benefits for a country are created. The creation of social enterprises may lead to the reduction in unemployment rates for a country, but also to the increase of employers' contributions. Also, women spend a great amount of their per capita income at various sectors of economy, as for instance health and education for their children, creating thus a significant social and economic impact (Hechavarria, Bullough, Brush & Edelman, 2019; Kapoor, 2019).

The investment in initiatives that may foster women's social entrepreneurship increasing their financial independence from women could constitute one of the most significant investment a country can make. The reduction in income inequality between the genders constitutes significant motivating power for the economic growth and poverty reduction in every society (Fabrizio, Fruttero, Gurara, Kolovich, Malta, Tavares & Tchelishvili, 2020). It is a reality that there is space for full gender equality in Scotland since the Scotland's Gender Equality Index was ranked 73 out of 100 (1 = no equality, 100 = full equality) in 2020 (Scottish Government, 2020). Women are more likely not to be working due to bring up their children leading them to a lower income compared to men (Čihák & Sahay, 2020; IMF, 2022). Alongside, wage gap between the two genders still exists, as 14.8% of women who have part-time jobs earn 33.5% less than men who work in a similar form of employment (Statista, 2021a). Remarkably, women constitute 75% of the workforce who works in part-time jobs in Scotland, whereas women earn £175.30 less than men every week (Statista, 2021a).

Women's social entrepreneurship contributes to women creating their own enterprise and consequently reducing unemployment (Anggadwita, Luturlean, Ramadani & Ratten, 2017). The reduction in unemployment for every country, in its turn, contributes to the reduction in social unemployment benefits and social policy from the country. Also, when a social enterprise is created and unemployed workers find a job, they are able to pay higher taxes receiving higher earnings improving its state welfare (Block, 2016; Hamermesh & Nottmeyer, 2016). In this way, we expect that the generated wealth may be increased for every country, increasing the GDP of every country. Therefore, the reduction in unemployment and poverty for every country is a basic requirement for its economic growth.

Of course, by being aware that social enterprises produce beyond economic value, also social value, they play a particularly catalytic role in the social cohesion of a country (Wevers, Voinea & de Langen, 2020). For instance, all of the women's social enterprises that have as a goal to help women create or develop an existing enterprise, do great work knowing that in this way the inequality between the number of enterprises men have and the number of enterprises women have, is reduced. Women, via their social enterprises, have the opportunity to learn how enterprises are run and gain access to a wide social network meeting and interacting with other women with common values. In this way, women may be inspired by other business women to run their own business improving their employability.

1.9   Challenges upon the creation of women's social enterprise

The challenges upon the creation of a women's social enterprise are multiple and require proper management and confrontation. First of all, women's social entrepreneurship is a special branch of social entrepreneurship as it is focused exclusively only on women who want or have already created a social enterprise. Many countries, however, are male-dominated and consequently the place of women is not the proper one. So, it is particularly difficult for women to create their own enterprise. Also, it is particularly difficult for the executives of the state mechanism from these countries to give emphasis and to support actions and activities for the promotion and reinforcement of women's social entrepreneurship. Also, in many countries, the potential businessmen are motivated due to their culture (i.e., individualistic cultures), to create a for-profit enterprise, than an enterprise with social impact (Mair & Schoen, 2007).

Alongside, it is obvious that in many countries, there is not an integrated institutional framework for the social enterprises and many times, the ambiguity that is created over this kind of entrepreneurship functions as a suppressive agent for the women who want to create their own enterprise (Lumpkin, Moss, Gras, Kato & Amezcua, 2013). Additionally, the lack of knowledge for the sense and the goals of social entrepreneurship constitutes one more challenge for many potential businessmen (Tracey, & Phillips, 2007). For this reason, education and updating for all citizens and mainly for women constitute significant conditions for the promotion of this kind of entrepreneurship.

Additionally, many women may not have developed certain digital skills which many times are necessary for the successful operation of an enterprise (Dixon, & Clifford, 2007). It is particularly significant to give emphasis on the development of women's digital skills in order to be able to respond efficiently to the contemporary digital challenges. The constant need of learning new digital skills could be vital throughout the life cycle of the new venture understanding different aspects of digitalisation, and using of social media (Olsson & Bernhard, 2021).

It is also true that many women come face to face with the sense of fear of a failure of their enterprise. This may be the outcome of a series of factors, as for instance lack of confidence, self-knowledge, or self- worth, but also various stereotypes concerning the woman's role in society. This is also connected with the balancing of professional and personal life and time which theoretically a woman should devote to her professional activities (Zerwas, 2019). All these stereotypes can have a negative effect on a woman's intention to create her own enterprise (Gupta, Turban & Bhawe, 2008).

Another challenge, which women who wish to create their own social enterprise face is to define the term "social enterprise", its economic but also its social value that is created via their social enterprise (Khervieux, Gedajlovic & Turcotte, 2010). Some illustrative questions that women are calling to answer include: Which is the social value that is created via a social enterprise? Can it be measured? If yes, how many will be benefited via the enterprise? Will the enterprise have also income? If yes, on what purpose will the income be available? Have any sponsors or investors been approached for the social enterprise? All these questions must be answered provided that the social enterprise wishes to be sustainable and develop in the future.

An additional challenge which women who may face a social or for-profit enterprise is the access to funding sources (Sinclair, Mazzei, Baglioni & Roy, 2018). Many times, investors find it difficult to be convinced on the sustainability of the idea and are suspicious towards the business plan of women entrepreneurs. This prejudice of theirs often leads them to not taking them so seriously as they should. This, however, has to be surpassed and only the sustainability of the idea to be examined.

Being also aware that networking is a particularly significant tool for the successful development of the enterprise, women entrepreneurs often face difficulty at building their own social net. Networking is particularly significant in the field of social enterprises, as the possibility is given to the entrepreneurs to have access to any sponsorship, investors and other funding sources that in the beginning of every enterprise play a particularly significant role (Dodgson, 2011). Moreover, it is also significant the fact that networking can be achieved in conferences and other events where in their beginning particularly, but also in their later development, women entrepreneurs should attend in order to enrich the network of their professional acquaintances. Many times, the saying "It does not matter what you know, but who you know" prevails.

Another challenge that is being particularly perceived in the underdeveloped countries, but also in the developed ones sometimes, is the incomplete education of women. It is true that the lack of education, therefore also lack of development of necessary for entrepreneurship abilities, leads to multiple problems, one of which is the creation of social enterprises (Marshall, 2011).

1.10   Obstacles upon creating women's social enterprise

The obstacles upon creating a social enterprise vary and constitute significant factors that influence the opening, but also the sustainability of a social enterprise. The obstacles of social entrepreneurship include the limited time, the many family obligations for bringing up children, the fear of failure, inexperience but also the limited support on funding sources or networking (Robinson, Mair & Hockerts, 2009). Alongside, many times the environment in which the social enterprise will become active plays a particularly significant role (Dacin, Dacin & Matear, 2010). More analytically, for instance, if a social enterprise is active in a developed economy like Australia, Austria, the United States of America and Sweden has far less possibilities to confront obstacles, compared with a social enterprise which is active in a developing or emerging economy as for instance Egypt, Bulgaria and Romania. That is, the external environment of a country can create obstacles in a social enterprise, making the everyday activity difficult in various ways. For instance, the corruption level of a country's economy plays a particularly significant role for the creation of a social enterprise. If, for instance, the corruption level in a country (usually developing) is particularly high, this can increase the period between the will to start a social enterprise and the actual start of the social enterprise.

It is true, in fact, that many times a lot of countries do not possess an organised economic context for the social enterprises, creating thus ambiguity for the institutional framework. Moreover, an unstable economic environment of a country can cause inability to the financial institutions to provide financing to social enterprises. The high educational level is also particularly significant, as it is observed that in countries where they do not possess the relevant knowledge, the goal and the vision of a social enterprise may not be understood.

1.11   Gap between women and men in relation to employment in the United Kingdom

By examining the employment of men and women in the United Kingdom from 2000 until 2019, we found that men's employment between 16 and 64 was 80, 3% for 2019, 8.3% more than women's employment for the same age group, reaching 72% (Statista, 2021b). In contrast with the gap between men's and women's employment in the United Kingdom which was set to 13.3% for 2000, with the men employed at a rate of 79.2% and women at a rate of 65.9% (Statista, 2021b). On the other side, unemployment in the United Kingdom for February 2019 was 4.9%, whereas the highest unemployment rate that has been registered in the United Kingdom was in the spring of 1984, which reached the rate of 11.9% (Statista, 2021b).

As far as the geographical distribution of unemployment is concerned, in February 2021, the highest unemployment rate was registered in London where it was set to 7.2%, which is higher than the average rate of unemployment in the United Kingdom which was set to 5% (Statista, 2021c). In the United Kingdom, unemployment, in the years that followed the economic crisis of 2008, was set between 5.1% in the beginning of 2008 and 8.5% in November 20011 (Statista, 2021d). However, after the peak of unemployment in November 2008, unemployment followed a downward trend, reaching 3.8% for many months in 2019 (Statista, 2021d). Interestingly, the coming of COVID-19 pandemic, stopped the downward trend of unemployment in the United Kingdom and in fact it led it to a significant raise, climbing up to 5% for many months in 2020 (Statista, 2021d).

As far as the number of self-employed in the United Kingdom is concerned, in February 2021 there were 2.8 million self-employed men, whereas significantly smaller was the number of self- employed women, reaching 1.5% million (Statista, 2021e). At an earlier time, the highest registration rate of self-employed men in the United Kingdom, was registered in September 2019, where the self-employed men reached 3.3 million, whereas the highest registration rate of self-employed women for the United Kingdom was registered before the coming of COVID-19 pandemic, reaching 1.7 million (Statista, 2021f).

1.12   Methodology of study

Our study is based on a multiple case study of seven social enterprises, and, therefore, is qualitative in nature (Siggelkow, 2007; Welch, Piekkari, Plakoyiannaki & Paavilainen-Mäntymäki, 2011). A similar methodology (i.e., multiple case study of seven social enterprises) has previously used in other social entrepreneurship studies (Tykkyläinen & Ritala, 2021), and it is also recommended in case studies research providing rich contextual data (Ravenswood, 2011). Indeed, the methods of case studies are considered as a widely used methodological approach in the field of social entrepreneurship as the field of social entrepreneurship grows and the researchers are engaged to different methodological approaches (Ulhoi, 2005; Mulloth, Kickul & Gundry, 2016; Pelucha, Kourilova & Kveton, 2017) aiming to deeper understand the interaction of phenomena and its context (Guercini & Ceccarelli, 2020). We deeply assessed secondary sources from the selected cases including websites, annual reports, corporate documents, sectoral reports, and social media coverage to provide full information for the selected social enterprises. The inclusion criteria for our selected social enterprises as cases studies in our study include (i) to be women-led, (ii) to have as their goal to reinforce women's entrepreneurship and also to help women create their own social enterprises or further develop their already existing social enterprises (therefore, they generate social impact and social value) and (iii) to be based (mainly) in Scotland (or in the UK, in general).

Case studies are especially useful for generating new ideas (Yin, 2013; Mulloth, Kickul & Gundry, 2016) although the strength of generalisability of case studies is weak (Bamberger, 2008). Therefore, generalisability should be avoided considering that our study is context sensitive paying attention to a specific country (Bamberger, 2008). Addressing other qualitative research methods (i.e., interviews, ethnography, focus groups) could be interesting revealing a deeper understanding of women-led social enterprises (Shah & Corley, 2006).

1.13 United Kingdom (a valuable context for investigation)

The United Kingdom seems to be a valuable national context for exploring social entrepreneurship for several reasons. First, 47% of social enterprises are led by women in the United Kingdom revealing the extent to which they grow considerably (Social Enterprise UK, 2021). Second, social enterprises in the United Kingdom seem to be quite optimistic for the future. Specifically, 60% of social enterprises in the United Kingdom are expected to hire staff in the next 1 year as well as 64% of social enterprises expect to grow their turnover during the same time period (GOV, 2021). Third, although the United Kingdom has been suffered by several exogenous shocks (i.e., Brexit, COVID-19), the British social enterprises seem to be more resilient compared to rest business demonstrating an optimistic behaviour for their future survival. Remarkably, 93% of Scottish social enterprises in the United Kingdom have been negatively affected by the COVID-19 pandemic although 42% of them had access to a Scottish Government funding in 2020 (Social Enterprise UK, 2021).

1.14 Key contributions of study

This study aims to investigate how key women led social enterprises in the United Kingdom help women create their own social enterprises or further develop their already existing social enterprises. This study is the first conducted in the United Kingdom exploring this type of social enterprises adopting a case studies analysis. Our study has mainly practical contributions. First, the identification of the key women led social enterprises operated in the United Kingdom may enable other social enterprises to identify their offered services, business models, and their scalability facilitating, and make optical decisions.

Remarkably, our case studies may also enhance the understanding of women led social enterprises regarding the key challenges that they are dealing with (i.e., resource-constraints, lack of digital skills, lack of confidence, self-knowledge or self- worth, stereotypes concerning the woman's role in society) and may hinder entrepreneurship. Therefore, it could draw the attention of policy makers to address some of the highlighted obstacles that women are dealing with during their entrepreneurial journey.

In addition, this study can be quite useful for future studies since it integrates insights from women-led social enterprises and their offered services in the British context formulating future paths for entrepreneurs who may be interested in setting up a new venture or scaling up their existing venture in the future. Fourth, the taxonomy, and the mapping of services provided by key women-led social enterprises has a significant potential contribution on social value creation fostering gender equality. Last but not least, our study reveals that government should be play a crucial role in fostering entrepreneurial spirit of women to be engaged to entrepreneurial activities contributing to job creation, which in turn, it may lead to economic growth of a country.

1.15 Conclusion

It is true that the significance of a social enterprise for every country should constitute a basic priority for all countries. The economic and social benefits with which a social enterprise is connected are multiple and a country that invests in social entrepreneurship can only benefit. However, the way towards the creation of social enterprises, many times is not easy, as social entrepreneurs come face to face with various obstacles, and they have to surpass them for the effective organisation and management of their social enterprise.

Of course, in a rapidly changing environment, the question for the social entrepreneurs is which business model they want to possess and which kind of value they want to create via their social enterprise (economic, social, environmental). Many times, the leading abilities of a social entrepreneur or the state framework in which they create the social enterprise form the business model of the social enterprise. Nevertheless, the field of social entrepreneurship and particularly the one of women's social entrepreneurship shows particularly great dynamics, as there is an increasing trend and will for introduction of motives for women to start their own enterprise. The reasons behind the institutionalisation of motives for the women's social entrepreneurship are many, among others, the gap reduction between the two genders as far as unemployment, salaries or the number of people who possess their own social enterprise are concerned.

In any case, we conclude that a social entrepreneur should consider some questions before creating his own social enterprise, as follows: How easy is for a social enterprise to create only social impact without having income from selling products or services? Which investment movements or strategic alliances the social enterprise owes to make in case it wishes to have a social impact only? How sustainable is such a business model? Which is the long-term business plan of the social enterprise and which its next movements?

Note

1 GDP refers to "*the income earned from production, or the total amount spent on goods and services*" (OECD, 2022).

2 Empirical part – case studies on women's social enterprises

2.1 Introduction

In this chapter, the selected women's social enterprises that are active and based in the United Kingdom will be presented. Interestingly, their main goal is to reinforce women's entrepreneurship and also to help women create their own social enterprises or further develop their already existing social enterprises.

2.2 Case Study 2a: The Association of Scottish Businesswomen (ASB)

2.2.1 Mission, vision and goals of ASB programme

ASB, which was founded in 1995, has as its goal to become the voice of all the women who own an enterprise in Scotland. ASB concerns all those women who work in enterprises, possess managerial positions or positions of responsibility, are self-employed or work in an organisation or an enterprise, regardless of the responsibility and experience level they have. ASB supports all the women from the aforementioned categories of employment, supporting them to achieve their goals. Its mission is to support these companies, to inspire them and to offer them networking with other companies and organisations. ASB encourages the personal and professional development of women who come from all kinds of activities, regardless of professional experience. The goal of ASB is to promote business opportunities by exchanging news among companies, developing networking among them and acknowledging their achievements and the implementation of their goals (The Association of Scottish Businesswomen, 2023a).

2.2.2 ASB programme services

ASB offers all its members a series of services, as for instance, access to groups, social media (i.e., Facebook, Twitter, Instagram, LinkedIn), networking with

DOI: 10.4324/9781003407249-3

other women from all kinds and extends of business industry, opportunities to share their news on social media, but also to write articles in them and to use the logo of the social enterprise. ASB also offers access to networking events with a special discount for the members of the programme, which aim at women's inspiration and their support during the creation or the development of their enterprise. More analytically, ASB has introduced an annual conference, weekends orientated to teaching leadership and the good way of living.

One of the most significant services of ASB programme is the annual awards "ASB National Business Awards" which provide free invitation to all the members of the programme and constitute an annual national recognition of the achievements and successes of social enterprises in Scotland. Alongside, ASB offers the enterprises which are its members access to various partners of the programme. For instance, the members of ASB programme have a subscription for the Council for Development and Industry (SCDI, Scottish Council for Development & Industry) which possesses a leading place on the development of sustainable economic perspectives for enterprises in Scotland, and organises various events for its members all the year around. Also, all ASB programme members have the opportunity to make their voice be heard through various researches in order to influence the governors to correct any distortions and obstacles relevant to women's entrepreneurship (The Association of Scottish Businesswomen, 2023b).

2.3 Case study 2b: Business Women Scotland (BWS)

2.3.1 Mission, vision and goals of WBS programme

Business Women Scotland (BWS) was founded 12 months ago and its goal is to help women and also to offer networking to its members. Its mission is to offer everything women who are occupied with business activities need and they are provided with a series of training courses to start or develop their own enterprise. For instance, a group of courses on various topics is offered by BWS, Mentoring from experts at industry, a monthly magazine for the communication of news, but also business awards as a recognition and promotion of the best women's enterprises every year. According to Lynne Kennedy, head of BWS programme: "Our goal, our vision is to provide women with support and to encourage them to make an innovating world, in a groundbreaking way. We want to acknowledge and celebrate women's entrepreneurship while alongside we create the agenda for equality" (Business Women Scotland, 2023a).

2.3.2 BWS programme services

More analytically, the subscription to BWS programme provides access to a series of services, as for instance, how to promote and develop your enterprise, law services, consulting services relevant to the creation and development of a business site of the enterprises, help at the development of social media, advice on access to new funding sources but also mentoring from the best professionals of the field (Business Women Scotland, 2023b, 2023c).

Also, a monthly magazine dedicated and orientated to women who deal with business activities is published online and communicates all its news with BWS members (Business Women Scotland, 2023d). Alongside, throughout the year various and useful for entrepreneurship courses are presented by experts of the field which aim to enrich their knowledge and to improve various abilities of the women who deal with entrepreneurship and are members of this programme. For instance, in the year 2021, comprehending the great ambiguity that existed in the external environment due to the pandemic, BWS programme offered most of its courses online and many of them orientated towards the effective confrontation of crises and challenges (Business Women Scotland, 2023e).

2.4   Case study 2c: Women's Enterprise Scotland (WES)

2.4.1 Mission, vision and goals of WES programme

Women's Enterprise Scotland (WES) was founded in 2011 and aims at the reinforcement of the Scottish economy via the development of women's enterprises. The enterprises that are owned by women reach 20% of the total of enterprises and contribute about 8.8 billion pounds to the national economy of the United Kingdom every year. It is noticeable, also, that women's entrepreneurship created about 230,000 new places of employment in the local society, contributing in this way crucially to the reduction in unemployment of Scotland. As far as the contribution of women's entrepreneurship to certain fields is concerned, it is characteristic that in the food and drinks industry, it contributed 5.6 billion pounds, in tourism 4.1 billion pounds and in the field of biological sciences 1.5 billion pounds (Women's Enterprise Scotland, 2023a).

The mission of WES is to support enterprises which are owned or managed by women, thus unlocking innovation and productivity and creating a positive impact on economy. The vision of WES is for Scotland to become a leading country at supporting women, providing them with equality at the access of opportunities and resources to create and develop their own enterprises (Women's Enterprise Scotland, 2023a).

The pursuit of WES is to encourage more and more women to dare create their own enterprise via the effective prediction of the needs of the market. The goal of WES is to double the number of enterprises that are owned or/and managed by women in the years to come, by doubling also the contribution of women's entrepreneurship to the national economy and to the creation of new places of employment. By reinforcing women's entrepreneurship, the gap that exists between the number of enterprises owned or/and managed by men and the number of enterprises owned or/and managed by women can be reduced.

2.4.2 WES programme services

The total of WES programme services is offered totally free to all the women who are thinking of creating their own enterprise, but also to those who want to develop more their already existing enterprise. WES, in collaboration with various ambassadors, inspires and supports them to start and then develop their own enterprise (Women's Enterprise Scotland, 2023b).

Also, WES provides the proper training to women who are its members in order to develop all those skills which are required in order to successfully respond to their organisation's requirements and function of their enterprises. Also, WES has created a digital centre of women's businesses (Women's Business Centre) which will be presented thoroughly later in the book, with the goal of building a community consisted of women who have created their own enterprise and probably wish to further develop their enterprise and also of women who want to create their own enterprise in the immediate future (Women's Enterprise Scotland, 2023c).

2.5   Case study 2d: Women's Business Centre

2.5.1 Mission, vision and goals of Women's Business Centre programme

Women's Business Centre is run by WES which is a non-profit business that has supported women's entrepreneurship since 2011. The Women's Business Centre has various supporters which support it via donations, as for instance, the Royal Bank of Scotland and the Crowdfunder UK. The mission of the Women's Business Centre is to help women locate the business opportunity, create and develop their business idea (Women's Business Centre, 2023a).

More analytically, the Women's Business Centre offers support to crucial issues for the sustainability of an enterprise, as for instance access to funding sources, the combination of professional and personal life, the support on social network and mentoring from experts of the field. The broader vision of Women's Business Centre is to help the women of Scotland unlock their business skills, have access to innovating technologies and help building the enterprises of the future. Alongside, the Women's Business Centre contributes to bridging the differences between men's and women's entrepreneurship, and also facilitates a broader strategy of "We can do it" for a sustainable economic development and equal opportunities for all (Women's Business Centre, 2023a).

2.5.2 Women's Business Centre programme services

The programme of Women's Business Centre offers access to a series of business news and articles, and access to network in Scotland but also to the rest of the world totally free for all men and women. Alongside, access via the website of the social enterprise to news and articles related to various funding sources of enterprises is provided, with support mechanisms for the enterprises and also mentoring from experts of the field. Also, there is a detailed guide on the website of the social enterprise related to the steps and the help a woman needs during the creation or development of an enterprise. There is support on the decision-making about location, the development of a business plan, the identification of a consultant, information about the laws and the legislation that is required for the establishment of an enterprise, the sales and promotional practices and actions that the enterprise will provide, the identification of digital skills that are required for the survival of enterprise, and information about networking events (Women's Business Centre, 2023b).

2.6   Case study 2e: Investing Women

2.6.1 Mission, vision and goals of investing women programme

The social enterprise Investing Women has as its goal to attract women who are interested in investing in newly established enterprises and up today, via this enterprise, "business angels" have invested in more than 21 enterprises. One of the enterprises in which money was invested is TC Biopharm, top enterprise of cancer and other diseases prevention which produces effective products for the early prevention of these diseases via a cellular innovation patent. Also, ScotBion which is a biotechnological enterprise of spirulina cultivation where, contrary to the conventional spirulina cultivators, uses a special light for its fast growth inside steel boxes. Another pioneer enterprise which has been funded by "business angels" is Envisioned which was founded at a small village near Innerleithen by the Scottish Fashion designer Alex Feechan and has as its goal to maintain the Scottish cultural heritage via the creation of traditional fabrics (Investing women, 2023a).

The Investing Women enterprise provides a supporting environment and urges women to invest in new and much promising enterprises and become the "business angels" of these enterprises. The mission of Investing Women programme is to train "business angels" how to be "smart investors". The members of Investing Women meet six times a year and welcome all those interested in becoming members of the social enterprise and have the opportunity to get in touch with the whole procedure for the first time. In each of these meetings, the attendees are given the possibility to meet two or three enterprises in which the members of Investing Women have already invested. These enterprises come from various fields and offer a vast experience and knowledge to the members who are part of this procedure (Investing women, 2023b).

2.6.2 Investing women programme services

The programme Investing Women, which is based on investments in women's enterprises, offers knowledge, training and support to potential "business angels" and helps them locate the proper investing opportunities. It is worth noticing that the consulting team of the programme Investing Women is possessed by such morality that allows them to use their knowledge and skills to support the investors properly. "Business angels" prefer to invest in enterprises that are based on Scotland and have at least one or more founding members that are women. Their investment ranges between £50k and £250k, but many times much money is invested, examining each case in particular. Beyond the aforementioned typical criteria which the enterprises have to meet in order to be funded by "business angels", it is necessary for the enterprises to have also a series of other criteria as for instance (a) to have innovative technology or business model, (b) the funding team should be constituted by more than one persons, (c) the business model of the product or service should be approved/checked, (d) to exist complete comprehension of the route the product or service will follow in the market and (e) there should exist the perspective of the product or service to expand in markets outside Scotland or the United Kingdom (Investing women, 2023c).

2.7 Case study 2f: Women in Banking and Finance (WiBF)

2.7.1 Mission, vision and goals of Women in Banking and Finance (WiBF)

The Women in Banking and Finance (WiBF) programme which was founded in 1980 aims at the reinforcement of the business spirit of its members, which is implemented by social network activities, the creation of development programmes and leadership programmes (Women in Banking and Finance, 2023a). WiBF has branches in Belfast, Bristol, London, Edinburgh, Glasgow, Birmingham and Manchester and offers access to activities to those who want to attend them, whether they are members of this organisation or not (Women in Banking and Finance, 2023b). Many of the activities are performed online, so the possibility is provided to those who wish to attend these activities at a later time. The mission of WiBF is to bridge the gap between men and women in the financial field in the United Kingdom. The vision of WiBF is that the financial field will offer equal opportunities to women whether they are employed, clients, entrepreneurs with the goal to "build" better enterprises for all (Women in Banking and Finance, 2023c).

2.7.2   Women in Banking and Finance (WiBF) programme services

WiBF offers a series of services to its members, with the goal to connect all the members via a common network, the challenge of adopting new innovating ideas and the inspiration of the community for change. WiBF has established annual awards for the reward of business excellence and of the achievements of the enterprises which are active in the business field. Additionally, WiBF offers mentoring to its members via a 6-month programme, providing access to experienced professionals of the financial field. A particularly significant service is also the networking of this organisation's members via development activities which are held during the year. Acclaimed professionals from the financial field share with the members all the experiences they have acquired from their professional life, providing useful information. Besides the experienced executives or the successful entrepreneurs of the financial field, courses and speeches are provided by other scientists of other fields. Trained psychologists explain, for instance, how psychological security affects the performance of the groups (Women in Banking and Finance, 2023d).

2.8   A "different and valuable" case study: Women's Business Station

Apart from the aforementioned social enterprises, our study presents an impactful social enterprise titled Women's Business Station (WBS) which unfortunately come to the end and closed in November 2022 due to not being able to source adequate funding for continuation. Remarkably, it raised the bar for equality, inclusion and diversity and operated in over 5 years supporting the socio-economic empowerment of over 1,000 women. The reason for including this impactful case study in our study is to show that when the social enterprises are not sustainable by finding enough funding (i.e., grants, sponsorships) overcoming their costs (i.e., operational, fixed, variable costs), they might deal with the chances of failure (Mantere, Aula, Schildt & Vaara, 2013).

This case study could be a valuable chance to present the main causes for entrepreneurial failure, in general. Indeed, entrepreneurial failure can be happened for several reasons including failure of external shareholders (i.e., lack of finding enough funding through grants, sponsorships), environmental disruptive phenomena (i.e., COVID-19 pandemic, energy crisis, economic crisis) or personal causes (i.e., lack of confidence, networks, mistakes and inexperience) (Cardon, Stevens & Potter, 2011; Smollan & Singh, 2021).

2.8.1 Mission, vision and goals of WBS programme

The mission of WBS programme was to increase the social-economic reinforcement of women via a series of activities, WBS programme aimed to build connected communities, by developing co-operations, innovating and creating opportunities which support women to succeed in their business goals. Alongside, the vision of WBS was to constitute the first stop of every women's enterprise to help it be created, built or developed in Scotland (Women's Business Station, 2021a).

The goals of WBS included among others include:

a   The increase of the social-economic reinforcement of women, with particular emphasis on those women who had difficulties with entrepreneurship in the past,
b   The creation of solutions and the confrontation of inequalities, by removing any obstacles that prevent the creation of enterprises,
c   The handing in of an annual training course relevant to business activities which create opportunities for women, cultivate their skills and improve their self-confidence and
d   The development of cooperation with local enterprises and experts via social networking.

In order to achieve the aforementioned goals and also the mission of the social enterprise, WBS had created three strategic orientations:

a   Education – by creating an annual educational plan with seminars, mentoring, coaching, and also all the necessary courses for a woman to acquire the knowledge needed to create or develop an enterprise (Women's Business Station, 2021a)
b   Law and financial courses, trade – by developing and supporting many commercial activities which include markets and e-commerce (Women's Business Station, 2021b), and
c   Talent – by giving the members of the programme the chance to participate in online promotions of products and services (Women's Business Station, 2021c, 2021d).

It is impressive that from 2017 to November 2022, WBS had helped more than 402 women who had participated in it. From these women, 130 have already created their own enterprise and 101 develop their existing enterprises. In this way, it is remarkable that for the same time period, more than 128 new places of employment had been created offering the local society an economic benefit worth of 4.1 million pounds (Women's Business Station, 2021e). Supporters of this programme were many companies and local agents, among which the Royal Bank of Scotland, Stedman, Ymindset, DC Thomson but also the Dundee and Angus Chambers Commerce (Women's Business Station, 2021f).

2.8.2 WBS programme services

The WBS programme offered many activities, online courses and speeches, laboratories and other activities. For the first 3 months, the WBS programme mostly invested in educating women who were members of the programme to understand basic concepts, as for instance what words coming from psychology mean: the word "Self-confidence" or the word "Self-improvement" and also words coming from finance as for instance the concept of "business angel". WBS programme, via fun activities, significantly helped new entrepreneurs to acquire the proper and required knowledge, through learning the business terminology which functions as a common glossary among entrepreneurs. Alongside, by knowing the significant role of networking, WBS programme brought in touch, via its various activities, all the women who participate in it. At the same time, WBS programme offered a series of courses, as for instance: "Product promotion", "Marketing and Communication", "Logistics and Finance", "Social Networks and Support Teams" and "Digital Means of Communication".

It is worth mentioning that, also, during the last days of the programme, interviews and questionnaires were held so as the management of the social enterprise to examine how much the women of the programme were helped to discover their emotions and to improve their knowledge on entrepreneurship.

2.9   Conclusion

Recapitulating all the case studies that were presented in the above unit, it is easily understood that the range of services which the women's social enterprises offer to women who wish to create their own enterprise and also to women who wish to develop their existing enterprise, is wide. On the table which will be presented next (see Table 2.1), are included all the social enterprises which were studied above and are examined according to some certain characteristics and also whether they offer some certain services. For instance, social enterprises are examined whether they offer to their members Training courses, Mentoring, Financial services, Networking or other Business awards. Also, it is examined whether the access to these services is provided for free, whether an annual subscription is required and if the corresponding amount of the subscription is defined. Finally, the criteria for someone to become a member of these social enterprises are examined.

Table 2.1 Case studies of women's social enterprises in the UK – A detailed comparison among them

Women's social enterprises	The Association of Scottish Businesswomen (ASB)	Business Women Scotland (BWS)	Women's Enterprise Scotland (WES)	Women's Business Centre	Investing Women	Women in Banking and Finance (WiBF)	Women's Business Station (WBS)
Training courses	Yes	Yes	Yes	Yes	Yes	Yes	Yes
Mentoring	No	Yes	No	No	Yes	Yes	Yes
Financial services	Yes	Yes	Yes	Yes	Yes	No	Yes
Networking	Yes	Yes	No	No	Yes	Yes	Yes
Business awards	Yes	Yes	No	No	Yes	Yes	No
Membership	£50 for the premium subscription and free for the basic subscription	£48 for a 6-month subscription and £96 for annual subscription			£350 for annual subscription	£72 for annual subscription (the members have free access to all the activities)/ the non-members usually pay £10 for every activity	£150 for annual subscription (for company creation) £200 for annual subscription (for development of an existing company £250 for annual subscription (for businesswomen who want to develop their networking)
Criteria for joining	The social enterprise/s should be owned by woman/women	- The social enterprise/s should be owned by woman/women - The social enterprise should have annual revenue (gross) £100k and more - The social enterprise should be active for at least 3 years	The social enterprise/s should be owned by woman/women	The social enterprise/s should be owned by woman/women	The social enterprise/s should be owned by woman/women	- The social enterprise/s should be owned by woman/women - To come from banking or financial field	The social enterprise/s should be owned by woman/women

Questions which refer to case studies

- Question 1

  How do you evaluate the vision, the mission and the goals of women's social enterprises? Do you believe there is perspective for these women's social enterprises to succeed and also to develop?

- Question 2

  Why some of the women's social enterprises chose to provide their services for free, while some others offer them for a fee?

- Question 3

  What it the strategic orientation of women's enterprises and which are their activities in order to accomplish their strategy?

- Question 4

  According to the international bibliography, social enterprises come up against many obstacles which are called to deal with. Which challenges do you believe they came up against the above social enterprises?

- Question 5

  How do you estimate the women's social enterprises are going to confront antagonism (if any in the field) maintaining their competitive advantage?

- Question 6

  Their up today strategic orientation do you believe is capable of maintaining or reinforcing their place in the field of social enterprises or should it be enriched or even changed?

- Question 7

  If you were a member of the Board of directors of any of the aforementioned women's social enterprises, which are you proposals for the strategic development of your social enterprise?

- Question 8

  Given the fact that networking plays a catalytic role for the sustainability of a social enterprise, what actions will you perform to increase your social network?

- Question 9

  How do you evaluate the development perspectives of women's social entrepreneurship today? In which countries do you believe it presents particular dynamics and in which countries less?

- Question 10

  Given the importance of the women's social enterprises which have as their goal to reinforce the business intention of women to start their own enterprise and also to develop the women's enterprises already existing, what other kinds of social enterprises would you suggest that might have a positive social impact?

3 Suggested activity plan for the reinforcement of women's entrepreneurship (social or for-profit enterprises)

3.1 Introduction

The suggested activity plan includes a series of activities which have as their goal to develop the abilities and skills of women entrepreneurs or of the potential women entrepreneurs and also to help them be aware of their emotions. These activities can play a catalytic role upon the discovery of unknown aspects of women's personality, heal any weaknesses or negative experiences of the past related to entrepreneurship and help them develop the strong but also necessary characteristics for the organisation and management of an enterprise. More analytically this programme includes the following activities.

3.2 Activity a: Awareness of emotions

Knowing the significant role of emotions during the business procedure, the introduction of the activity of awareness of important emotions is suggested, as for instance, the emotions of sorrow, joy, fear and others which affect the whole frame of mind of a person who deals with entrepreneurship. When you observe and discover your emotions, you are able to understand what is necessary to be improved, what your weaknesses are, but also which the strong elements of your frame of mind are. Perhaps, many times, not only one emotion prevails, but more, when you make the effort to discover them (Fernández-Pérez, Montes-Merino, Rodríguez-Ariza & Galicia, 2019).

However, it is needed to be understood that it is never wrong to feel one and only emotion mostly. It is significant to discover it, aiming at its improvement in case it has a negative effect on one of your actions, you wouldn't wish it to have. Can you name the emotion you feel? Is it more than one? What are you thinking when you are overwhelmed by this emotion? Can you change it? Have you ever felt that it can affect some of your actions? If yes, which actions? When answering to all these crucial questions, someone is able to handle this frame of mind better.

DOI: 10.4324/9781003407249-4

3.3   Activity b: Blob tree exercise

Blob tree exercise was created by psychologist Pip Wilson and aims at identifying the emotions and up to a point, identifying the social layer of each emotion. More analytically, every person (figure) of the tree depicts a different emotion and has a different place on the tree. However, it is particularly significant to use the term "blob" because the figures depicted do not have gender, nationality and whatever else may affect the outcome of the exercise. The tree can be the company in which someone works, his family, a sports team or a group of people with whom the person who does the activity interacts. This activity can be repeated at various periods of time and at various occasions (Glenn, 2016).

3.4   Activity c: Letting your light shine

According to Alexandra House (2015), the way for the "cure" is considered to be unique for each woman who has been abused in the past. This activity has as its goal to trace these wounds in order to "cure" them. More analytically, the following presented steps have been originally developed by Kate Cavett (N/A), and have detailed presented from Alexandra House (2015), and include a series of certain steps, as they are presented analytically:

3.4.1 Step 1: Name the abuse

The aim of this step is to trace all those experiences which women thought at first they were "normal" but later realised they were harmful for themselves, with intense negative effect on their mental state. This step starts by convincing every woman to start talking to people she trusts. The people whom a person usually trusts are friends, family or the wider close family environment.

3.4.2 Step 2: Trace security

As soon as a woman has traced abuse, it is particularly significant to create a personal plan in order to keep herself away from future harmful behaviours from third parties. It is very important at this stage that all the fears and the past situations at which the woman found herself face to face with some harmful behaviours to be traced. The goal of this step is to locate the places where every woman feels secure. These places vary from woman to woman and can be home, workplace or anywhere else. In this way, every woman can create a plan that she can turn to when she faces her current fears.

3.4.3 Step 3: Gather (human) resources

Many times, women come up against abuse by themselves, but it is much easier to come up against it with the support of third parties. This support can come from people or organisations. More analytically, support can be found in friends, family or generally people whom the woman trusts. This support can also be found in organisations that specialise at women's psychological support and perform excellent work. The goal of seeking human resources is that every woman can develop her own network of people or enterprises where she feels secure in, in order to go back to it if and when she is confronted with some insulting behaviour in the future. In this way, the psychological and mental health of every woman will be ensured.

3.4.4 Step 4: Choose a different better path

As soon as you trace and gather the human resources needed to confront difficult situations, it is significant to decide to choose a better path for yourself. Decide on how you want to see yourself after some years and with whom you want to develop a personal or/and a professional contact and relationship.

3.4.5 Step 5: Define the meaning of love

It is particularly significant to think what the word "love" means to you. Many times we do not have the time to think what really makes us happy. Which are the situations of which we draw joy and pleasure? Who are the persons we have combined with joyful situations and events? Mapping people and situations that are combined with joy constitutes a particularly significant process for the creation of a new definition of the word "love".

3.4.6 Step 6: Get to know yourself

As soon as you define the meaning of love for yourself, it is particularly significant to meet someone whom perhaps you did not have the opportunity to meet in the past and is none other than yourself. However, at this stage, someone should not be critical with himself, as the goal of this stage is to trace the strong and the weak points of every person. The elements of someone's character that he does not like are at his discretion to change them. This stage also helps a person come closer to truth by getting to know himself.

3.4.7 Step 7: Develop the limits of your (mental) health

It is very important at this stage to trace what the limits of your mental health are. It is important to know up to what extend you can allow the other's behaviour affect you and how he can behave to you. For instance, respect is required at all cases and must be considered self-evident by all.

3.4.8 Step 8: Mourn your "past" emotions

It is particularly significant, as soon as you find yourself in a safe emotional environment, to "mourn" some of your past emotions that made you feel anger or uncomfortable in the past. Mourning past emotions is a process where you take your time to expel the emotions you felt in the past that kept you away from tranquillity and calmness.

3.4.9 Step 9: Accept where you are and determine where you want to go

What happened in the past could be wrong, simply now you know the reason. You are also aware of your emotions, the past ones and the present. You also know that only if you determine new destinations and situations, you will move forward and discover new emotions that will be connected with joy, your mental peace and security.

3.4.10 Step 10: Let the light come inside you to be developed

Many times, it is necessary to say positive words for our-self and encourage us, by stressing the positive elements of our character. It is also significant to have cured any wounds from the past in order to let the light come inside our-self and help us develop.

3.5 Activity d: Write down only your positive thoughts in a diary

An activity which also helps at the improvement of self-awareness and the improvement of mental state is the writing down of all those simple, positive facts on everyday basis (Tod, Hardy & Oliver, 2011). It is particularly significant to write down the positive activities so that the decoding of a person's character can be done and the location of all the positive activities throughout the day, so as to increase them. The removal of negative emotions that is perhaps accompanied with certain situations constitutes significant motivation for the beginning of decoding the emotions. As it is depicted further on, it is particularly significant for women to answer to questions such as for instance: When did I feel strong for the last time? When was that time? Under what conditions do I feel great? When was the last time I felt pleasure? What mistakes did I make in the past? Did I learn from my mistakes? Which characteristic of my personality makes me unique? Have I invested in this characteristic?

3.6 Activity e: Make your emotions visible – the "Iceberg of Anger"

The goal of this activity is to help women manage their anger, and also their emotions in general. Via the "Iceberg of Anger" the possibility is given for all the visible emotions that are on the surface and above the borderline of the "iceberg" to be written down and in fact are the emotions we see. However, the possibility is also given for all the invisible emotions which are under the surface of the "iceberg" to be written down and in fact are all those emotions we do not see and contribute to the externalisation of behaviours and emotions we see (Benson, 2016). In this way, women are able to think under which situations they were driven to show anger behaviour, and which other emotions drove them to anger expression. The location of the motivation forces of anger and of the under lying situations that contribute to its expression are particularly significant. The location of negative emotions that exist under the "iceberg" and contribute to anger expression can constitute a starting point for the proper anger management. For instance, negative emotions when we are angry can be underlying such as guilt, anxiety, stress, irritation, distrust, insecurity, shame, grief, exhaustion, nervousness and many others.

3.7   Conclusion

Although some of the aforementioned activities may occur in some social or for-profit enterprises, it is particularly significant for all of the enterprises to be included, creating thus an integrated plan of reinforcement of women's entrepreneurship. The goal of these activities is to help women discover their true self and who they truly are, but also to trace their strong elements and which characteristics of their personality need improvement. Only in this way can anyone understand what he does right and what needs to be improved in order to achieve individual and organisational goals.

4 Policy recommendations

4.1 Introduction

In this chapter, an integrated set of activities and actions are presented that is required to be implemented at a panhellenic level, and in any other country in the world with the goal of reinforcing women's entrepreneurship. The comprehension of the term "social entrepreneurship" and its benefits for the society and economy of every country are considered to be prerequisites for the effective planning and also for the successful implementation of this long-term plan. Alongside, it is suggested to every country, to study the best women's social enterprises that are active in this country or other countries and decode the components of their success, with the goal, these characteristics to constitute a model for the designing of a national strategy for the social enterprises.

4.2 Creation of an integrated long-term plan for social enterprises

It is particularly important the policy makers of every country – either a developed market or an emerging market – to create and launch an integrated plan for the social entrepreneurship. Reinforcement of women's social entrepreneurship in particular has to constitute a separate strategic orientation for many countries, reducing thus the employment gap between men and women in every society. The vision of every country should be to eliminate the wage gap between the two genders and any other relevant discrimination. A society where every woman should have the same opportunities with a man should constitute the vision of every country.

More analytically, it should be created tax and financial motives for the creation of a social enterprise. It is also imperative at a European level to create information campaigns referring to the sense of a social enterprise and also to the benefits which is connected. Every country should increase the number of the social enterprises which are active in her and consider them as a separate branch of enterprises, facing their key challenges.

DOI: 10.4324/9781003407249-5

It is particularly important that a separate platform should be created that would include all the social enterprises, their vision, their mission, their main activities, their funding sources, their assets, their financial results but also the number of people who have been benefited by them. That is, there should be absolute transparency from every social enterprise revealing the total number of enterprises that are active in every country. While in many developed countries it already exists, in some less developed and mostly in many developing countries, it has not been implemented yet. Also, the creation of such a platform will help the potential investors and "business angels" to invest in social enterprises included in the platform. For instance, it is particularly significant for someone who wants to invest in a social enterprise to be persuaded about the transparency of the social enterprise. Alongside, the introduction of social entrepreneurship courses at primary or secondary education is also recommended for fostering entrepreneurial spirit. The familiarisation with the sense of social entrepreneurship especially from a young age is considered to be particularly significant, as young men and women decide at the age of 18, the professional path they wish to follow. Students should know well the different kinds of entrepreneurship as an alternative career path that it might be interesting for them if they want to follow it. The emphasis especially on social entrepreneurship via some university institutions is also suggested, as most university curricula are orientated to profit- entrepreneurship. By introducing courses, workshops, and seminars of social entrepreneurship to the curricula of university studies, the opportunity is given to the students to be aware of this kind of entrepreneurship, its characteristics, the challenges it faces, enabling them to compare it to for-profit entrepreneurship.

It is also suggested that an annual competition of the best women's enterprise for every country should be launched. It is also suggested that this competition could be accompanied by money award for the three best social enterprises. Notably, the best social enterprises should be rewarded by society, signifying thus, the emphasis it gives to this branch. These awards could be awarded by the most acclaimed in the social enterprises field but also by the competent state agencies. The acknowledgement of the efforts of the social enterprises constitutes a particularly significant initiative of every state, as it constitutes, many times, the motivating power for the social enterprises to continue seamlessly and with the same zeal their social work.

It is also recommended, the creation of a panhellenic conference for the women's social enterprises, with international repute speakers from the academic field, but also from the field of social enterprises. In this conference, all-even the new-social enterprises that managed via their mission and activities to be distinguished through the year will be presented. These social enterprises can constitute an example for the potential social enterprises, but also for the already existing social enterprises. Additionally, in this conference, women of social enterprises who did not manage to correspond to the increasingly uncertain external environment and closed their social enterprise will have a possibility to participate in the conference and share their experiences. In this way, the mistakes that possibly have been made will be presented with the goal of being avoided from other future social entrepreneurs. This pan-hellenic conference can become a networking place for the women's social enterprises, comprehending the significant role of network in the sustainability of a social enterprise. Moreover, in this conference potential investors can be found who want to be informed about their actions and also their social impact, and also invest in them. Many times, investors want to meet social enterprises closely, to be informed about their actions, but also their social impact before investing their money in them. Alongside, investors are keen many times on meeting the founder/s and the CEOs of the social enterprises and fully comprehend the vision of his/their social enterprise.

Many countries have also given particularly emphasis on for- profit enter-prises, putting aside the importance of social enterprises and their catalytic role to social cohesion and the economy of a state. For this reason, the crea-tion of an integrated manual with the steps required for the creation of a social enterprise is particularly significant. This integrated manual will be available for all the citizens who want to establish a social enterprise. Also, a consult-ant from the responsible Ministry maybe assigned to some social enterprises who are dealing with problems with the goal of reducing the time of their establishment.

Additionally, given the lack of digital skills of many women, and their right of creating their own social enterprise, the state should provide them funded training courses and opportunities with the goal to familiarise them with notions relevant to entrepreneurship in the new digital era. Given that digital skills are required for technology adoption and are considered as a main challenge for small enterprises (Dimitratos & Kyriakopoulos, 2022; Kyriakopoulos, 2022), women's training on entrepreneurship field should constitute of an utmost importance priority of every state.

The state, beyond women's training, should also provide access to fund-ing sources to women who want to start their own social enterprise. More analytically, every year a bigger part of the annual state budget and a bigger part of National Strategic Reference Framework (NSRF) (in those countries members of the European Union) should be provided to social enterprises, as the funding of social enterprises can operate as a starting capital for many newly established social enterprises in order to achieve their mission. Many times, women, although they have the idea for a social enterprise, do not have the capitals to implement it themselves. For this reason, they seek for capitals from outside funding sources. It is a fact that at their start, many social enter-prises face cash flow problems, trust problems from donators, problems of limited access to other funding sources and for this reason they turn to bank loans or government grants. During their first years until they are set in the field in which they are active, social enterprises face more problems than they face later on, due to lack of cash flow and also many times lack of trust from funders.

Simplifying also, many procedures can surely contribute to bureaucracy reduction which constitutes a significant challenge for many states. Also, the emphasis on digital transformation of many countries and the development of digital skills is required for the reinforcement of the culture of social entrepreneurship of many countries. The creation of social enterprises "with just one click" can constitute a significant motive for the creation of more social enterprises. It is also suggested the funding for creating the websites of all the social enterprises, with the goal to promote their social work widely and thus to increase the number of the potential sponsors/ investors. The creation of competitive websites will have to be a significant priority for many social enterprises, as it constitutes the first and many times the only connection of the social enterprise with the sponsors/ donators.

4.3   Conclusion

The development of every economy and of every society can be achieved via the reinforcement of women's social entrepreneurship. In some countries more actions may be needed, while in others, actions of a smaller scale are needed. In any case, however, all countries should comprehend the benefits of women's social entrepreneurship. Via various case studies which were presented in this book, it was realised that a developed country as the one of the United Kingdom has created the suitable framework for the creation of these women's social enterprises, which can constitute an example for many other countries, too.

What is impressive, from the case studies presented, is that they are about social enterprises which have been created and managed by women, but also, they address to women too, comprehending the significant role they can play in the society and the economy of every country. The emphasis on women's entrepreneurship which aims at providing services to women shows particular dynamics these days, given the increased women's role in society.

The weaknesses of the external environment and many pathogeneses of states that are many times unable to respond to the increasing needs of the social whole, constitutes the contribution of social enterprises particularly significant these days. Reinforcement of the culture of women's entrepreneurship should come to the fore by many countries and the creation of motives for the increase of the creation of this kind of social enterprises should be placed in the immediate plan of many states. It is imperative to create a single institutional framework for the social enterprises which will adjust and solve all the problems with which the social entrepreneurs come up.

References

Alexandra House (2015). Letting your light shine – Teens healing from abuse. Available at: https://www.alexandrahouse.org/letting-your-light-shine-teens-healing-from-abuse/ (Accessed: 12 December 2022).

Alter, S. K. (2006). Social enterprise models and their mission and money relationships. In A. Nicholls (Ed.), *Social entrepreneurship: New models of sustainable social change* (pp. 205–232). New York: Oxford University Press.

Anggadwita, G., Luturlean, B. S., Ramadani, V., & Ratten, V. (2017). Socio-cultural environments and emerging economy entrepreneurship: Women entrepreneurs in Indonesia. *Journal of Entrepreneurship in Emerging Economies,* 9 (1), 85–96.

Apostoli (2023a). Greeting of his beatitude archbishop of Athens and all Greece Ieronymos II. Available at: https://mkoapostoli.com/poioi-imaste/%cf%87%ce%b1%ce%b9%cf%81%ce%b5%cf%84%ce%b9%cf%83%ce%bc%cf%8c%cf%82- %ce%b1%cf%81%cf%87%ce%b9%ce%b5%cf%80%ce%b9%cf%83%ce%ba%cf%8c%cf%80%ce%bf%cf%85/ (Accessed: 12 January 2023).

Apostoli (2023b). The mission of Apostoli. Available at: https://mkoapostoli.com/ (Accessed: 21 January 2023).

Apostoli (2023c). Facilities. Available at: https://mkoapostoli.com/%ce%b7-%ce%b4%cf%81%ce%ac%cf%83%ce%b7-%ce%bc%ce%b1%cf%82/%ce%ba%ce%bf%ce%b9%ce%bd%cf%89%ce%bd%ce%b9%ce%ba%ce%ad%cf%82-%ce%b4%ce%bf%ce%bc%ce%ad%cf%82/ (Accessed: 26 January 2023).

Apostoli (2023d). Our mission. Available at: https://mkoapostoli.com/ (Accessed: 30 January 2023).

Austin, J., Gutierrez, R., Ogliastri, E., & Refcco, E. (2006). *Gestión efectiva de emprendimientos sociales. Lecciones extraídas de empresas y organizaciones de la sociedad civil en Iberoamérica* (SEKN, ed.). México, DF: Banco Interamericano de Desarrollo.

Bamberger, P. (2008). Beyond contextualization: Using context theories to narrow the micro-macro gap in management research. *Academy of Management Journal,* 51 (5), 839–846.

Bansal, S., Garg, I., & Sharma, G. D. (2019). Social entrepreneurship as a path for social change and driver of sustainable development: A systematic review and research agenda. *Sustainability,* 11, 1091. https://doi.org/10.3390/su11041091

Barro, J. R. (2017). *Macroeconomic theory.* Athens, OH: Paschalidis Publications.

Benson, K. (2016). The anger iceberg. Available at: https://www.gottman.com/blog/the-anger-iceberg/ (Accessed: 29 January 2023).

Block, J. (2016). Corporate income taxes and entrepreneurship activity. *IZA World of Labor*. https://doi.org/10.15185/izawol.2577

Bocken, N. M. P., Short, S. W., Rana, P., & Evans, S. (2014). A literature and practice review to develop sustainable business model archetypes. *Journal of Cleaner Production*, 65, 42–56.

Business Women Scotland (2023a). Welcome to business women Scotland voice representing women in business. Available at: https://www.bwsltd.co.uk/ (Accessed: 20 January 2023).

Business Women Scotland (2023b). Programme for growth. Available at: https://www.bwsltd.co.uk/programme-for-growthv (Accessed: 15 January 2023).

Business Women Scotland (2023c). Mentoring. Available at: https://www.bwsltd.co.uk/mentoring-programme (Accessed: 1 January 2023).

Business Women Scotland (2023d). Business women Scotland magazine. Available at: https://www.bwsltd.co.uk/magazine (Accessed: 12 February 2023).

Business Women Scotland (2023e). News. Available at: https://www.bwsltd.co.uk/news (Accessed: 14 January 2023).

Cajaiba-Santana, G. (2014). Social innovation: Moving the field forward: A conceptual framework. *Technological Forecasting and Social Change*, 82, 42–51.

Cardon, M. S., Stevens, C. E., & Potter, D. C. (2011). Misfortune or mistakes? Cultural sensemaking of entrepreneurial failure. *Journal of Business Venturing*, 26 (1), 79–92. Doi:10.1016/j.jbusvent.2009.06.004.

Carvalho, S. W., Sen, S., de Oliveira Mota, M., & de Lima, R. C. (2010). Consumer reactions to CSR: A Brazilian perspective. *Journal of Business Ethics*, 91 (2), 291–310.

Chell, E. (2007). Social enterprise and entrepreneurship: Towards a convergent theory of the entrepreneurial process. *International Small Business Journal*, 25 (1), 5–26.

Choi, N., & Majumdar, S. (2013). Journal of business venturing social entrepreneurship as an essentially contested concept: Opening a new avenue for systematic future research. *Journal of Business Venturing*, 29 (3), 1–14.

Čihák, M., & Sahay, R. (2020). Finance and inequality. Staff Discussion Note 20/01. International Monetary Fund, Washington, DC.

Çingitaş, Y., & Sati, Z. E. (2015). Economic and social benefits that can be obtained by a combination of innovation and corporate entrepreneurship activities in Turkish companies. *Procedia, Social and Behavioral Sciences*, 195, 1129–1137.

Dacin, P. A., Dacin, M. T., & Matear, M. (2010). Social entrepreneurship: Why we don't need a new theory and how we move forward from here. *Academy of Management Perspectives*, 24 (3), 37–58.

Dimitratos, P., & Kyriakopoulos (2022). COVID-19 crisis challenges and responses: Evidence from selected Greek SMEs. In H. Etemad (Ed.), *Small and medium sized enterprises and the COVID-19 response: Global perspectives on entrepreneurial crisis management*. Cheltenham: Edward Elgar, 323–345.

Dixon, S. E., & Clifford, A. (2007). Eco- entrepreneurship: A new approach to managing the triple bottom line. *Journal of Organizational Change Management*, 20 (3), 326–345.

Dodgson, M. (2011). Exploring new combinations in innovation and entrepreneurship: Social networks, Schumpeter, and the case of Josiah Wedgwood (1730–1795). *Industrial and Corporate Change*, 20 (4), 1119–1151.

Ebrahim, A., & Rangan, V. K. (2014). What impact? A framework for measuring the scale and scope of social performance. *California Management Review*, 56 (3), 118–141.

Elkington, J. (1998). *Cannibals with forks*. Gabriola Island, BC: New Society Publishers.

Fabrizio, S., Fruttero, A., Gurara, D., Kolovich, L., Malta, V., Tavares, M. M., & Tchelishvili, N. (2020). Women in the labor force: The role of fiscal policies. IMF Staff Discussion Note 20/03. International Monetary Fund, Washington, DC.

Fallon, N. (2014). What is corporate social responsibility? *Business News Daily*, February 27, 2014.

Fernández-Pérez, V., Montes-Merino, A., Rodríguez-Ariza, L., & Galicia, P. E. A. (2019). Emotional competencies and cognitive antecedents in shaping student's entrepreneurial intention: The moderating role of entrepreneurship education. *International Entrepreneurship and Management Journal*, 15 (1), 281–305.

Freeman, R., & Reed, D. (1983). Stockholders and stakeholders: A new perspective on corporate governance. *California Management Review*, 25 (3), 88–106.

Gatti, L., Caruana, A., & Snehota, I. (2012). The role of corporate social responsibility, perceived quality and corporate reputation on purchase intention: Implications for brand management. *The Journal of Brand Management*, 20 (10), 65–76.

Ghalwash, S., Tolba, A., & Ismail, A. (2017). What motivates social entrepreneurs to start social ventures? An exploratory study in the context of a developing economy. *Social Enterprise Journal*, 13 (3), 268–298.

Giudici, A., Combs, J. G., Cannatelli, B. L., & Smith, B. R. (2020). Successful scaling in social franchising: The case of impact hub. *Entrepreneurship Theory and Practice*, 44 (2), 288–314.

Glavas, A., & Mish, J. (2015). Resources and capabilities of triple bottom line firms: Going over old or breaking new ground? *Journal of Business Ethics*, 127 (3), 623–642.

Glenn, L. (2016). The "Blob tree" psycho-emotional test. Διαθέσιμοστο:https://glennlimthots.wordpress.com/2016/03/11/the-blob-tree-psycho-emotional-test/ (Accessed: 18 December 2022).

Godfroid, C., Otiti, N., & Mersland, R. (2022). Employee tenure and staff performance: The case of a social enterprise. *Journal of Business Research*, 139, 457–467.

GOV (2021). Small business survey. GOV. Available at: https://www.data.gov.uk/dataset/efa5133a-ad72-47a3-aef9-b4f8ab385a0c/small-business-survey (Accessed: 13 January 2023).

Gravells, J. (2012). Leaders who care - the chief executives' view of leadership in social enterprises: Natural aptitude versus learning and development. *Human Resource Development International*, 15 (2), 227–238.

Grenier, P. (2009). Social entrepreneurship in the UK: From rhetoric to reality? In R. Ziegler (Ed.), *An introduction to social entrepreneurship: Voices, preconditions, contexts* (pp. 174–206). Cheltenham: Edward Elgar.

Guercini, S., & Ceccarelli, D. (2020). Passion driving entrepreneurship and lifestyle migration: Insights from the lutherie of Cremona. *Journal of International Entrepreneurship*, 18 (3), 373–392.

Gupta, V. K., Turban, D. B., & Bhawe, N. M. (2008). The effect of gender stereotype activation on entrepreneurial intentions. *Journal of Applied Psychology*, 93 (5), 1053–1061.

Haigh, N., Walker, J., Bacq, S., & Kickul, J. (2015). Hybrid organizations: Origins, strategies, impacts and implications. *California Management Review*, 57 (3), 5–12.

Hall, M., Millo, Y., & Barman, E. (2015). Who and what really counts? Stakeholder prioritization and accounting for social value. *Journal of Management Studies*, 52 (7), 907–934.

Hamermesh, D. S., & Nottmeyer, O. K. (2016). *Evidence-based policy making in labor economics: The IZA world of labor guide*. London, England; New York: Bloomsbury Academic.

Hechavarria, D., Bullough, A., Brush, C., & Edelman, L. (2019). High - growth women's entrepreneurship: Fueling social and economic development. *Journal of Small Business Management*, 57 (1), 5–13.

Huybrechts, B., & Nicholls, A. (2012). Social entrepreneurship: Definitions, drivers and challenges. In C. K. Volkmann, K. O. Tokarski & K. Ernst (Eds.), *Social entrepreneurship and social business* (pp. 31–48). Germany: Gabler Verlag.

Ilac, E. J. D. (2018). Exploring social enterprise leadership development through phenomenological analysis. *Social Enterprise Journal*, 14 (3), 268–288.

International monetary Fund (IMF) (2022). IMF strategy toward mainstreaming gender. *IMF*. Available at: https://www.imf.org/en/Topics/Gender (Accessed: 2 February 2023).

Investing women (2021a). Case studies. Available at: https://www.investingwomen.co.uk/our_portfolio/findra/ (Accessed: 13 January 2023).

Investing women (2023b). Support. Available at: https://www.investingwomen.co.uk/support/ (Accessed: 22 January 2023).

Investing women (2023c). Pitch. Available at: https://www.investingwomen.co.uk/pitch/ (Accessed: 24 January 2023).

Ithaca (2023a). About Ithaca. Available at: https://ithacalaundry.gr/about/ (Accessed: 1 February 2023).

Ithaca (2023b). Impact. Available at: https://ithacalaundry.gr/impact/ (Accessed: 1 January 2023).

Kapoor, S. (2019). Entrepreneurship for economic and social empowerment of women: A case study of self-help credit program in Nithari Village, Noida, India. *Australasian Accounting, Business & Finance Journal*, 13 (2), 123–142.

Kate Cavett. (N/A). Kate Cavett's healing wheel. Available at: http://www.katecavett.com/resources/HealingWheel.pdf (Accessed: 12 February 2022).

Khervieux, C., Gedajlovic, E., & Turcotte, M. F. B. (2010). The legitimization of social entrepreneurship. *Journal of Enterprising Communities: People and Places in the Global Economy*, 4 (1), 37–67.

Kim, S. (2019). The process model of corporate social responsibility (CSR) communication: CSR communication and its relationship with consumers' CSR knowledge, trust, and corporate reputation perception. *Journal of Business Ethics*, 154 (4), 1143–1159.

Kyriakopoulos, P. (2022). Challenges in digital entrepreneurship. In M. Munoz (Ed.), *Digital entrepreneurship and the global economy*. New York: Routledge, 11–20.

Lumpkin, G. T., Moss, T. W., Gras, D. M., Kato, S., & Amezcua, A. S. (2013). Entrepreneurial processes in social contexts: How are they different, if at all? *Small Business Economics*, 40 (3), 761–783.

Mair, J., & Schoen, O. (2007). Successful social entrepreneurial business models in the context of developing economies: An explorative study. *International Journal of Emerging Markets*, 2 (1), 54–68.

Manolopoulos, D., Salavou, H., Papadopoulos, A., & Xenakis, M. (2022). Strategic decision-making and performance in social enterprises: Process dimensions and the influence of entrepreneurs' proactive personality. *Entrepreneurship Research Journal*, 1–45. https://doi.org/10.1515/erj-2021-0147

Mantere, S., Aula, P., Schildt, H., & Vaara, E. (2013). Narrative attributions of entrepreneurial failure. *Journal of Business Venturing*, 28 (4), 459–473. Doi:10.1016/j.jbusvent.2012.12.001.

Marques, J., & Dhiman, S. (2020). *Social entrepreneurship and corporate social responsibility*. Cham: Springer.

Marshall, R. S. (2011). Conceptualizing the international for-profit social entrepreneur. *Journal of Business Ethics*, 98 (2), 183–198.

McWilliams, A., & Siegel, D. (2001). Corporate social responsibility: A theory of the firm perspective. *Academy of Management Review*, 26 (1), 117–127.

McWilliams, A., Siegel, D., & Wright, P. (2006). Corporate social responsibility: Strategic implications. *Journal of Management Studies*, 43 (1), 1–18.

Mishra, S., & Suar, D. (2010). Does corporate social responsibility influence firm performance of Indian companies? *Journal of Business Ethics*, 95, 571–601.

Mizrahi, T., & Rosenthal, B. B. (2001). Complexities of coalition building: Leaders successes, strategies, struggles, and solutions. *Social Work (New York)*, 46 (1), 63–78.

Mulloth, B., Kickul, J. R., & Gundry, L. K. (2016). Driving technology innovation through social entrepreneurship at Prezi. *Journal of Small Business and Enterprise Development*, 23 (3), 753–767.

OECD (2022). Gross domestic product (GDP). OECD. Available at: https://data.oecd.org/gdp/gross-domestic-product-gdp.htm (Accessed: 23 January 2022).

Ohana, M., & Meyer, M. (2010). Should I stay or should I go now? Investigating the intention to quit of the permanent staff in social enterprises. *European Management Journal*, 28 (6), 441–454. https://doi.org/10.1016/j.emj.2010.06.007

Olsson, A. K., & Bernhard, I. (2021). Keeping up the pace of digitalization in small businesses - Women entrepreneurs' knowledge and use of social media. *International Journal of Entrepreneurial Behaviour & Research*, 27 (2), 378–396.

Osterwalder, A., Pigneur, Y., Bernarda, G., & Smith, A. (2014). *Value proposition design: How to create products and services customers want*. Hoboken, NJ: Wiley.

Park, B. I., Chidlow, A., & Choi, J. (2014). Corporate social responsibility: Stakeholders influence on MNEs' activities. *International Business Review*, 23 (5), 966–980.

Park, E., Kim, K. J., & Kwon, S. J. (2017). Corporate social responsibility as a determinant of consumer loyalty: An examination of ethical standard, satisfaction, and trust. *Journal of Business Research*, 76, 8–13.

Park, Y. W., & Park, Y. J. (2021). *Corporate social responsibility and entrepreneurship for sustainability: Leading in the era of digital transformation*. Singapore: Springer.

Pelucha, M., Kourilova, J., & Kveton, V. (2017). Barriers of social entrepreneurship development - A case study of the Czech Republic. *Journal of Social Entrepreneurship*, 8 (2), 129–148.

Peredo, A. M., & McLean, M. (2006). Social entrepreneurship: A critical review of the concept. *Journal of World Business*, 41, 56–65.

Phills, J. A., Jr., Deiglmeier, K., & Dale, M. T. (2008). Rediscovering social innovation. *Stanford Social Innovation Review*, 6 (4), 34–43.

Portales, L. (2019). *Social innovation and social entrepreneurship: Fundamentals, concepts, and tools*. Cham: Springer International Publishing.

Ravenswood, K. (2011). Eisenhardt's impact on theory in case study research. *Journal of Business Research*, 64 (7), 680–686.

Rawhouser, H., Cummings, M., & Newbert, S. L. (2019). Social impact measurement: Current approaches and future directions for social entrepreneurship research. *Entrepreneurship Theory and Practice*, 43 (1), 82–115.

Robinson, J. A., Mair, J., & Hockerts, K. (2009). *International perspectives on social entrepreneurship*. Houndmills, Basingstoke & New York: Palgrave Macmillan.

Sachs, J., Schmidt-Traub, G., Kroll, C., Lafortune, G., & Fuller, G. (2019). *Sustainable development report 2019*. New York: Bertelsmann Stiftung and Sustainable Development Solutions Network (SDSN).

Santos, F. M. (2012). A positive theory of social entrepreneurship. *Journal of Business Ethics*, 111, 335–351.

Sastre-Castillo, M. A., Peris-Ortiz, M., & Danvila-Del Valle, I. (2015). What is different about the profile of the social entrepreneur? *Non-Profit Management & Leadership*, 4 (Summer), 41–50.

Scottish Government (2020). Scotland's gender equality index 2020. Available at: https://data.gov.scot/genderindex/gender-equality-index-2020.html (Accessed: 23 January 2022).

Shah, S. K., & Corley, K. G. (2006). Building better theory by bridging the quantitative-qualitative divide. *Journal of Management Studies*, 43 (8), 1821–1835.

Shedia (2023). Profile of diogenis NGO. Available at: https://www.shedia.gr/about-us/ (Accessed: 11 January 2023).

Siggelkow, N. (2007). Persuasion with case studies. *Academy of Management Journal*, 50 (1), 20–24.

Sinclair, S., Mazzei, M., Baglioni, S., & Roy, M. J. (2018). Social innovation, social enterprise and local public services: Undertaking transformation? *Social Policy and Administration*, 52 (7), 1317–1331.

Sjödin, D., Parida, V., Jovanovic, M., & Visnjic, I. (2020). Value creation and value capture alignment in business model innovation: A process view on outcome-based business models. *The Journal of Product Innovation Management*, 37 (2), 158–183.

Smith, L. G. (2014). *Impact assessment and sustainable resource management* (2nd ed.). New York: Routledge.

Smollan, R., & Singh, S. (2021). How social entrepreneurs respond to enterprise failure. *Journal of Social Entrepreneurship*, vol. ahead-of-print, no. ahead-of-print, 1–25.

Social Enterprise UK (2021). No going back - State of social enterprise survey 2021. Social Enterprise UK. Available at: https://knowledgecentre.euclidnetwork. eu/2022/01/12/european-social-enterprise-monitor-report-2020-2021-2/ (Accessed: 2 February 2023).

Statista (2021a). A statista dossierplus on inequality in the UK. Available at: https://www-statista-com.ezproxy.lib.gla.ac.uk/study/89363/inequality-in-the-uk/ (Accessed: 3 January 2023).

Statista (2021b). Unemployment in the UK. Available at: https://www-statista-com.ezproxy.lib.gla.ac.uk/study/21287/uk-unemployment-statista-dossier/ (Accessed: 23 January 2023).

Statista (2021c). Unemployment rate in the United Kingdom in July 2021, by region. Available at: https://www.statista.com/statistics/297167/uk-regional-unemployment-rate/ (Accessed: 12 January 2023).

Statista (2021d). Unemployment in the United Kingdom - Statistics & facts. Available at: https://www.statista.com/topics/1989/unemployment-in-the-united-kingdom/ (Accessed: 18 January 2023).

Statista (2021e). Number of self-employed workers in the United Kingdom from May 1992 to July 2021. Available at: https://www.statista.com/statistics/318234/united-kingdom-self-employed/ (Accessed: 24 January 2023).

Statista (2021f). Number of self-employed workers in the United Kingdom from May 1992 to July 2021, by gender. Available at: https://www.statista.com/statistics/318458/self-employment-in-the-uk-by-gender/ (Accessed: 28 January 2023).

Tate, W. L., Ellram, L. M., & Kirchoff, J. F. (2010). Corporate social responsibility reports: A thematic analysis related to supply chain management. *Journal of Supply Chain Management*, 46 (1), 19–44.

Teasdale, S. (2012). What's in a name? Making sense of social enterprise discourses. *Public Policy and Administration*, 27 (2), 99–119.

The Association of Scottish Businesswomen (2023a). About us. Available at: https://www.asb-scotland.org/about-us (Accessed: 13 January 2023).

The Association of Scottish Businesswomen (2023b). ASB membership resources. Available at: https://www.asb-scotland.org/member-resources (Accessed: 1 February 2023).

Tod, D., Hardy, J., & Oliver, E. (2011). Effects of self-talk: A systematic review. *Journal of Sport & Exercise Psychology*, 33, 666–687.

Tracey, P., & Phillips, N. (2007). The distinctive challenge of educating social entrepreneurs: A postscript and rejoinder to the special issue on entrepreneurship education. *Academy of Management Learning & Education*, 6 (2), 264–271.

Tykkyläinen, S., & Ritala, P. (2021). Business model innovation in social enterprises: An activity system perspective. *Journal of Business Research*, 125, 684–697.

Ulhoi, J. P. (2005). The social dimensions of entrepreneurship. *Technovation*, 25 (8), 939–946.

Waddock, S. A., & Post, J. E. (1991). Social entrepreneurs and catalytic change. *Public Administration Review*, 51 (5), 393.

Welch, C., Piekkari, R., Plakoyiannaki, E., & Paavilainen-Mäntymäki, E. (2011). Theorising from case studies: Towards a pluralist future for international business research. *Journal of International Business Studies*, 42 (5), 740–762.

Wevers, T., Voinea, H., & de Langen, C. L. (2020). Social entrepreneurship as a form of cross-border cooperation: Complementarity in EU border regions. *Sustainability (Basel, Switzerland)*, 12 (20), 8463.

Women Act (2023a). About women act. Available at: https://women-act.org/about/ (Accessed: 28 January 2023).

Women Act (2023b). Our work. Available at: https://women-act.org/our-work/ (Accessed: 29 January 2023).

Women Act (2023c). Our vision. Available at: https://women-act.org/about/ (Accessed: 29 January 2023).

Women Act (2023d). No more manels. Available at: https://women-act.org/no-more-manels/ (Accessed: 30 January 2023).

Women's Business Centre (2023a). Starting up? We're here to help. Available at: https://womensbusinesscentre.com/ (Accessed: 20 January 2023).

Women's Business Centre (2023b). What is the women's business centre? Available at: https://womensbusinesscentre.com/what-is-the-womens-business-centre/ (Accessed: 12 February 2023).

Women's Business Station (2021a). Our mission. Available at: https://www.businessstation.co.uk/our-mission/ (Accessed: 1 January 2021).

Women's Business Station (2021b). Enterprise programmes. Available at: https://www.businessstation.co.uk/enterprise-programmes/ (Accessed: 4 January 2021).

Women's Business Station (2021c). Mentoring. Available at: https://www.businessstation.co.uk/?page_id=169 (Accessed: 23 January 2021).

Women's Business Station (2021d). Mentoring. Available at: https://www.businessstation.co.uk/?page_id=300 (Accessed: 19 January 2021).

Women's Business Station (2021e). The future. Available at: https://www.businessstation.co.uk/the-bigger-picture/ (Accessed: 25 January 2021).

Women's Business Station (2021f). Empowerment partners. Available at: https://www.businessstation.co.uk/empowerment-partners/ (Accessed: 30 January 2021).

Women in Banking and Finance (2023a). Who we are. Available at: https://www.wibf.org.uk/discover/who-we-are (Accessed: 29 January 2023).

Women in Banking and Finance (2023b). Our locations. Available at: https://www.wibf.org.uk/discover/our-locations (Accessed: 29 January 2023).

Women in Banking and Finance (2023c). What we offer. Available at: https://www.wibf.org.uk/discover/what-we-offer (Accessed: 26 January 2023).

Women in Banking and Finance (2023d). Individual membership. Available at: https://www.wibf.org.uk/discover/personal-membership (Accessed: 19 January 2023).

Women's Enterprise Scotland (2023a). Strengthening the Scottish economy through women's enterprise. Available at: https://www.wescotland.co.uk/ (Accessed: 18 January 2023).

Women's Enterprise Scotland (2023b). Training. Available at: https://www.wescotland.co.uk/training (Accessed: 11 January 2023).

Women's Enterprise Scotland (2023c). National women's business centre. Available at: https://www.wescotland.co.uk/national-women-s-business-centre (Accessed: 14 January 2023).

Wu, Y. J., Wu, T., & Sharpe, J. (2020). Consensus on the definition of social entrepreneurship: A content analysis approach. *Management Decision*, 58 (12), 2593–2619.

Yin, R. K. (2013). *Case study research: Design and methods*. Thousand Oaks, CA: Sage Publications.

Yunus, M., Moingeon, B., & Lehmann-Ortega, L. (2010). Building social business models: Lessons from the Grameen experience. *Long Range Planning*, 43 (2), 308–325.

Zahra, S. A., Gedajlovic, E., Neubaum, D. O., & Shulman, J. M. (2009). A typology of social entrepreneurs: Motives, search processes and ethical challenges. *Journal of Business Venturing*, 24 (5), 519–532.

Zerwas, C. S. (2019). *Work-life balance and women's entrepreneurship: An exploration of influencing factors. Contributions to management science*. Cham: Springer International Publishing.

Index

Printed in the United States
by Baker & Taylor Publisher Services